The Black Arc...

THE
AMBASSADORS
OF DEATH

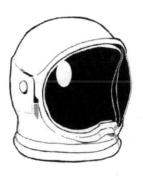

By LM Myles

Published March 2016 by Obverse Books

Cover Design © Cody Schell

Text © LM Myles, 2016

Range Editor: Philip Purser-Hallard

LM Myles would like to thank Philip Purser-Hallard for his patience and editorial skill.

To Mum, for introducing me to **Doctor Who** all those years ago

CONTENTS

OVERVIEW

Serial Title: *The Ambassadors of Death*

Writer: David Whitaker (credited), Malcolm Hulke and Trevor Ray (uncredited)

Director: Michael Ferguson

Original UK Transmission Dates: 21 March 1970 – 2 May 1970

Running Time: Episode One: 24m 33s

Episode Two: 24m 39s

Episode Three: 24m 38s

Episode Four: 24m 37s

Episode Five: 24m 17s

Episode Six: 24m 31s

Episode Seven: 24m 32s

UK Viewing Figures: Episode One: 7.1 million

Episode Two: 7.6 million

Episode Three: 8.0 million

Episode Four: 9.3 million

Episode Five: 7.1 million

Episode Six: 6.9 million

Episode Seven: 6.4 million

Regular cast: Jon Pertwee (Dr Who), Caroline John (Liz Shaw), Nicholas Courtney (Brigadier Lethbridge-Stewart)

Recurring Cast: John Levene (Sergeant Benton)

Guest Cast: Ronald Allen (Ralph Cornish), Robert Cawdron (Taltalian), John Abineri (General Carrington), Ric Felgate (Van Lyden/Astronaut), Michael Wisher (John Wakefield), Cheryl Molineaux (Miss Rutherford), Ray Armstrong (Grey), Robert Robertson (Collinson), Dallas Cavell (Quinlan), Bernard Martin (Control Room Assistant), Juan Moreno (Dobson), James Haswell (Corporal Champion), Derek Ware (UNIT Sergeant), William Dysart (Reegan), Cyril Shaps (Lennox), Gordon Sterne (Heldorf), Steve Peters (Lefee/Astronaut), Neville Simons (Michaels/Astronaut), Max Faulkner (UNIT Soldier), John Lord (Masters), Tony Harwood (Flynn), James Clayton (Private Parker), Joanna Ross (Control Room Assistant), Carl Conway (Control Room Assistant), Roy Scammell (Technician), Peter Noel Cook (Alien Space Captain), Peter Halliday (Aliens' Voices), Geoffrey Beevers (Private Johnson)

Antagonists: General Carrington, Reegan

Novelisation: *Doctor Who: The Ambassadors of Death* by Terrance Dicks. **The Target Doctor Who Library** #121

Responses:

'In need of a major re-evaluation, *The Ambassadors of Death* benefits from a multi-layered script and spooky spacesuited aliens. It also contains one of the series' finest climaxes...'

[Paul Cornell, Martin Day and Keith Topping , *The Discontinuity Guide*, p115]

'*The Ambassadors of Death* is a rather interesting thriller set in the near future, like *The Invasion* the year before [...] a throwback to the more leisurely, some might say rambling, stories of the black and white era.'

[Lance Parkin, 'Something Took off from Mars...', *Matrix* #52]

SYNOPSIS

Episode 1

Mars Probe 7, a British mission to Mars, loses contact during its exploration phase, and makes the return journey in radio silence.

Seven months after it leaves Mars another spacecraft, Recovery 7, is sent to retrieve the two-strong crew from Earth orbit. During the rendezvous – observed from Space Centre by Controller **Ralph Cornish** and UNIT's **Brigadier Lethbridge-Stewart**, and on the television by **the Doctor** and **Liz Shaw**, courtesy of presenter **John Wakefield** – contact is also lost with Recovery 7's single astronaut. At the same time an exchange of transmissions is detected between the capsule and Earth's surface – specifically an abandoned warehouse in London. UNIT raid the location, but armed men, led by **Carrington**, hold them off while they send a final transmission. One man surrenders while Carrington escapes.

At Space Centre the Doctor and Liz attempt to decode the signal, but are first hampered and then threatened at gunpoint by Cornish's computer expert, **Dr Taltalian**.

Episode 2

The Doctor refuses to hand over the tape of the transmission to Taltalian, who escapes, frustrated, from Space Centre. UNIT's sole prisoner from the warehouse standoff is uncommunicative, but the Doctor tricks him into revealing his military background before he too escapes, released by an unknown rescuer. The Brigadier suspects that their mysterious antagonists have inside knowledge,

9

and takes his concerns to **Sir James Quinlan**, the official in charge of the British space programme – who we learn is harbouring Taltalian.

Meanwhile, Recovery 7 re-enters the Earth's atmosphere, landing in southern England. Its occupants refuse to communicate or open the capsule, so it is transported back to Space Centre (being briefly hijacked en route by Carrington's men, but recovered by the Doctor).

Episode 3

When opened, the capsule proves to be empty, although its interior is flooded with radiation. Learning that the astronauts were extracted by a security patrol who visited the hangar earlier, the Brigadier and the Doctor once again confront Sir James. Quinlan introduces them to Carrington – in actuality General Carrington, a former Mars astronaut and head of the new Space Security Department. His men have been working to contain the three new arrivals, who are allegedly contaminated by an unknown and 'highly contagious' form of radiation.

The astronauts themselves – or at least three spacesuits and their occupants, who seem to need massive doses of radiation to survive, and weaken in its absence – are being held at Carrington's facility, but before the Doctor can see them they are abducted by a murderous criminal, **Reegan**. On their way to the underground bunker he's taking them to, they fatally irradiate the two men riding with them.

The Doctor guesses that the real astronauts are still aboard Mars Probe 7. While he works to repair the Recovery 7 capsule, Liz is lured to Hertfordshire to examine the irradiated bodies, but is cut off en route and chased by armed men.

Episode 4

Liz is caught and taken to Reegan's bunker, where a semi-captive scientist named **Dr Lennox** is looking after the space-suited individuals. Dr Taltalian brings them fresh supplies of a radioactive isotope, and Reegan gives him a time-bomb to use against the Doctor, who is attempting to decode radio transmissions recorded by the false astronauts' previous captors. When decoded, the radio transmissions reveal blueprints for a one-way translation machine, of a kind which Taltalian has built previously and supplied to Reegan.

Taltalian uses the bomb, but Reegan has set it to explode instantly. Taltalian is killed, but the Doctor survives. He volunteers to pilot a second recovery mission to retrieve the real astronauts from Mars Probe 7, which is still in orbit. Carrington – who claims that the two irradiated henchmen were foreign agents, and appears to have evidence backing this up – wants him stopped. Sir James eventually realises that the only way is to tell the Doctor the truth, but he will only do this in person.

Meanwhile Reegan uses Taltalian's translator to threaten the false astronauts. He blackmails them into attacking Space Centre in search of an equivalent translation device, and then Sir James's ministry, killing Quinlan with their deadly touch before he can speak to the Doctor.

Episode 5

At Liz's urging, Dr Lennox escapes from Reegan's bunker and turns himself in to UNIT, insisting on speaking to the Brigadier. Cornish defies Carrington and insists that the recovery mission will go ahead, with the Doctor as its pilot. Reegan and his unseen employer agree that the former will deal with the Doctor, the latter with Lennox.

Lennox is killed in his cell with the isotope, apparently by a UNIT soldier, before he can tell the Brigadier what he knows. Reegan sabotages the new recovery rocket's fuel mix, nearly killing the Doctor on launch, but Recovery 7 successfully gains Earth orbit and docks with Mars Probe 7. Before the Doctor can board it, however, a gigantic UFO appears on a collision course.

Episode 6

Aboard the alien spaceship, the Doctor finds the three missing astronauts alive and well, but hypnotised. He speaks to the vessel's **Captain,** and learns that the three aliens on Earth were sent there as Ambassadors by prior agreement – although the Doctor is certain Earth's authorities are unaware of this fact. Carrington attends a special meeting in Geneva , to commend to the Security Council its 'moral duty' of blowing the alien craft up.

The Doctor returns safely to Earth, but is abducted from Space Centre's decontamination chamber by Reegan, who takes him to the bunker where one of the increasingly desperate alien captives has shown Liz its face. Reegan keeps the Doctor alive, against instructions, hoping that he will build him a fully functional translator which will help him use the Ambassadors to commit crimes of his own. They are interrupted by Reegan's employer, General Carrington himself, who now considers that his 'moral duty' lies in shooting the Doctor.

Episode 7

Carrington admits that he met the alien species during his own visit to Mars, where they inadvertently killed one of his fellow astronauts. With the help of Quinlan (who wanted only public recognition and was not involved in the deeper conspiracy) he arranged for the ambassadorial visit, so that he could discredit the aliens and ensure a war between them and Earth. While Reegan stages a raid on an isotope factory with two of the aliens, Carrington returns to Space Centre with the third, who he intends, with Wakefield's help, to unmask on worldwide live TV.

The Doctor builds Reegan a working translator, but is also able to use it to send out a powerful SOS signal. Carrington seizes control at Space Centre, but the Brigadier escapes and rescues the Doctor. With the help of the two remaining Ambassadors, they break back into Space Centre and place Carrington under arrest. The Doctor leaves Liz and Cornish to handle the diplomatic exchange of the Ambassadors for the missing astronauts, and goes back to his attempts to repair the TARDIS.

INTRODUCTION

It's so easy to imagine *The Ambassadors of Death* (1970) [1], and the rest of **Doctor Who**'s original seventh season, as a rather brilliant BBC cult classic of the 1970s, mostly forgotten today, but still very well regarded by those who've seen it. '**Doctor Who**?' its fans would say, 'well, it's all right, I suppose, but I prefer my television a little more sophisticated. Have you ever seen **Season Seven**? No? Well, it's this show about a scientist who saves the world from strange, sometimes alien, threats by being terribly clever. He's got an assistant, and a police box... no, no, it's nothing like **Doctor Who**, don't be silly!'

Of course, one of the most wonderful things about **Doctor Who** is that it can be any genre it likes. It can even take what we regard as its most fundamental concept – the brilliant man in the magic box who has adventures all through time and space – and strip it out. It can say, 'Actually, no, no more magic box for you. You're stuck. Right here on Earth, and in the one time.' And it's still **Doctor Who**.

The 1970 season enjoys an enviable reputation in fandom: it's regarded as one of the most consistently good years in the show's history, and it's rare to find a fan of 20th-century **Doctor Who** who doesn't have at least one of its four stories in their Top 20 List. This season is also a landmark for **Doctor Who** in many ways. It's the first to be filmed in colour, there's a new Doctor, new companion, and a new format. Behind the scenes things are also in flux, as one of the most influential and successful partnerships in the show's history begins, when Barry Letts and Terrance Dicks take over as producer and script editor.

---

[1] Henceforth *Ambassadors* in the text.

Dicks, however, wasn't completely happy with what he was left with by the outgoing team, script editor Derrick Sherwin and producer Peter Bryant. In his view, as stated in the commentary track on *Ambassadors*, they'd left him with two big changes to the show, both of them terrible: the Doctor was stuck on Earth, and the stories were excessively long. Dicks began dismantling both these concepts the next year, switching to more stories with four parts, and getting the Doctor off Earth again, but for season seven, he was stuck with both. Certainly, one can appreciate his point of view in the long term – you can't keep a show that's about adventures in time and space stuck in a single time and space indefinitely – but for a season or two, it works.

Pick any story, any episode, in season seven and it's easy to see why this year remains so well regarded, decades later. It's got its own particular style and confidence, a taste for realism, and grit, a maturity that marks it out as unique amongst **Doctor Who**. I'm a fan of the silly: I enjoy puns, and unconvincing blobby aliens, and Tom Baker at his most prat-falling absurd. Season seven is anything but silly. It's a tone that couldn't survive for long, and as a fan I wouldn't want it to. **Doctor Who**, at its heart, is a childish creation. It relies on wonder, curiosity, and imagination. It wants you to believe that there is a strange old alien with a time machine who can go anywhere in time and space and have exciting adventures. That's the foundation of the series, and yet in season seven, it's stripped away; in keeping with the more adult tone of the year, we are no longer asked to believe such a fantastic conceit.

Instead we have a scientist, who is employed by a paramilitary organisation to assist in defending the Earth against extraordinary and unusual threats. The man is undoubtedly brilliant, and his

15

assistance essential in keeping the planet safe, but even his remarkable assistant, Doctor Elizabeth Shaw, doubts him when it comes to the extraordinary claims he makes regarding the police telephone box he keeps in his laboratory.

OPENING MOVES

Season seven bursts on screen with brand-new flashy opening titles that make full use of the switch to colour television. The mysterious black-and-white swirls of the William Hartnell and Patrick Troughton eras are gone, and in their place is a time vortex of riotous colour, bright and vibrant. Mystery has been exchanged for strangeness; discovery swapped for adventure.

The seven episodes of *Ambassadors* also have a unique twist in their opening titles, different from all other **Doctor Who** stories: each episode begins with a short prologue, reprising the cliff-hanger of the previous episode (except in episode 1, which gives us a prelude to the whole adventure), before we're flung back into the technicolour time vortex to finish off the opening title sequence. Two words fly at us: 'THE AMBASSADORS' ... then a 'ping' gunshot sound effect and 'OF DEATH' appears below, in a much larger font size. The credited story writer, David Whitaker[2], and the episode number follow on with the remains of the theme tune. It's rather fun, though I wish the gunshot sounded just a little less cartoony.

---

[2] Whitaker, a prolific **Who** scriptwriter since *The Edge of Destruction* (1964), had trouble adjusting to the series' new formula and bowed out after writing three episodes, although he continued to be credited. Trevor Ray revised episode one, while Malcolm Hulke (who had written the immediately preceding story, *Doctor Who and the Silurians* (1970, hereafter *The Silurians* for convenience's sake) as well as co-writing two scripts for Patrick Troughton's Doctor), revised episodes two and three and wrote episodes four to seven based on Whitaker's outline. Script Editor Terrance Dicks and Director Michael Ferguson also contributed to the final scripts. (Sullivan, Shannon Patrick, 'The Ambassadors of Death'.)

Just as important in making a good first impression is the title of the story itself. There's a pulp sci-fi feel to many **Doctor Who** story titles – *The Tomb of the Cybermen* (1967), *Terror of the Autons* (1971), *The Caves of Androzani* (1984) – one which I'm heartily in favour of, and if I were to make a list of Best **Doctor Who** story titles (lists being a popular pastime with many a **Doctor Who** fan) that sort of title would make a strong showing. The very best, however, happen when two instantly accessible concepts are juxtaposed. That means no one-off monster names (sorry, *The Macra Terror* (1967)), no planets (apologies, *The Androids of Tara* (1978)) and nothing that is just plain silly (*The Deadly Assassin* (1976), indeed. As opposed to...?). There's something timelessly brilliant about *An Unearthly Child* (1963), or *The Stones of Blood* (1978). Whatever one thinks of the stories themselves, the titles provoke a vivid imagining of what sort of adventure the Doctor and Co are about to embark upon.

The Ambassadors of Death falls into this category (it had the far less intriguing working titles of 'The Invaders from Mars' and 'The Carriers of Death'). There's many a **Doctor Who** title that promises death or terror or some such in the title, but few are paired with so intriguing a word as 'ambassadors.' Who are these ambassadors? Why do they bring death, and not peace, or at least a spot of diplomacy before they start with the killing? Are they the cause of death, or do they merely herald its arrival? One could fairly accuse a fair number of story titles as being a bit lazy, or unimaginative, but here we have one that is in keeping with the pulpy sci-fi tradition, while still showing a thoughtfulness that will permeate the rest of the story.

Ambassadors utilises a technique in its opening minutes that will become much more ubiquitous in the Russell T Davies era of **Doctor Who**: the journalist John Wakefield delivers his news reports regarding the progress of the Mars mission straight to camera. We'll see this again with the then-fictional 'BBC Three' news reports in *The Dæmons* (1971), and with BBC journalist Alex Macintosh reporting on the events of *Day of the Daleks* (1972), before Trinity Wells becomes a recurring newscaster in the early days of 21st-century **Who**. It's easy to see why this technique appealed. It not only allows a good reason for an exposition dump, but it gives an immediacy and relevance to the events we're seeing. If it's being reported on the telly, it feels important, even if we are, hopefully, in 2016, media-savvy enough that we realise not everything of importance is reported on television, and just because something's on television it doesn't mean it's important.

Wonderfully, while we're watching what's going on in mission control, and are listening to updates from Wakefield, so is the Doctor. Initially dismissive of what's going on, he gets drawn in and ends up sitting down, leaning in toward the telly, with a cup of tea, rather intrigued as to what the Recovery rocket is going to find on Mars Probe 7.

THE POWER OF THREE

Doctor Who began with a four-person TARDIS and a family dynamic. With the departure of Barbara and Ian that changed so that for the next five or so years, Team TARDIS was mostly a trio. Normally, the trio would be pretty weighted towards the Doctor being the most powerful character: he has knowledge and experience far in excess of his companions', and he has a time machine. In season seven, however, things are a little more balanced: the Doctor has lost some of his knowledge, the TARDIS has been disabled, and he is an alien exiled to human society. On the other sides of the triangle are Liz Shaw and Brigadier Lethbridge-Stewart, both powerful characters in their own right. Liz is a brilliant scientist, with the knowledge and skill to face the threats of this season even if the Doctor wasn't around, and the Brigadier is a smart, capable, high-ranking soldier with the resources and firepower of an international military organisation to back him up.

This sort of three-person team is a much-beloved trope in fiction, with the most famous and successful example in science fiction being seen in **Star Trek** (1966-69), with Kirk, Spock and McCoy. There we see a trope that's become known in popular culture as 'the Freudian trio'[3], which assigns Freud's concepts of the id, ego, and superego to a trio of characters: Spock is the rational, logical one; McCoy is the emotional, impulsive one; and Kirk is the balance that reconciles the other two. In this season of **Doctor Who**, we have a rather more complex Freudian trio, as it twists two ways, but in both, Liz Shaw is always the bridge in between.

---

[3] 'Freudian Trio'. TV Tropes.

In the opening scenes of the story, as the plot is established and the characters introduced, the first lines of conflict are drawn – between military and scientific, fear and curiosity, thirst for wealth and thirst for knowledge – some of which will be explored via the Freudian trio of the three main characters.

The Brigadier we see in *Ambassadors* is a smart, effective soldier. It's clear that he's out of his depth with most of the science, but he's not stupid. The questions he asks are intelligent and precise, ones worthy of a lay person who's no fool, and they allow the audience to stay informed about what's going on: when contact is lost with the Recovery 7 rocket on its eventual return, he very reasonably asks if something's wrong, and is reassured by the Doctor that contact is always lost in the last few seconds before landing. The Brigadier also realises what it means when the Recovery 7 rocket is coming down to Earth at 20,000 miles per hour. Of course, everyone in the Space Centre knows what it means, but having the Brigadier there allows someone to actually say it without anyone looking stupid – this isn't his field, and he's looking for reassurance that something can be done as much as stating what's obvious to everyone else[4]. We get to enjoy the Brigadier in the role of the intelligent companion again when the Doctor is in orbit, and a giant alien spaceship is on a collision course with him. He sounds agitated while Ralph Cornish, the head of the Space Centre, trained and experienced in the dangers of space travel, maintains his customary cool[5].

---

[4] *The Ambassadors of Death* episode two.
[5] Episode six.

Sadly, an often-stated criticism of season seven is that between them the Doctor and Liz Shaw are so smart that there's no-one to ask questions so the audience can understand what's going on. It's nonsense — if it's a science question, the Brigadier is there; if it's about the unknown, it's all new to Liz; and if you're a decent writer, surely, **surely** you can't be so terrible at your job that you need a character you consider unintelligent onscreen so you can get the exposition in. Indeed, one of the joys of *Ambassadors* is no-one is left carrying the idiot ball, which only heightens the tension of the conflicts between the characters.

The Brigadier we see in *Ambassadors* is a long way from responding to every alien threat with 'five rounds rapid'[6]. He's the reasonable, relatable military figure here, unwilling to attack without cause, who acts as a counterpoint both to the Doctor's scientific approach, and to General Carrington's belligerent war-mongering. We see his military authority and expertise used to actually further the investigation of who's behind the kidnapping of the Ambassadors, rather than as a punchline. He's also responsible for personally rescuing the Doctor twice in this story, and takes part in several gunfights, at one point coolly facing a man aiming a revolver at his head at point-blank range. A classic cliffhanger in episode four has the Doctor examining the body of Sir James Quinlan, unaware that an Ambassador is reaching towards him, hand outstretched, about to kill him with its deadly touch. He only survives because the Brigadier runs in, guns blazing, and distracts the Ambassador's attention. There's also a rather grim scene of the Brigadier under arrest, and being marched away along a dark tunnel by two

---

[6] As he does in *The Dæmons*.

22

soldiers. But this is Lethbridge-Stewart at his finest, and despite the fact that there are two guards, and that he's walking in front of them, unarmed, he manages to take them both out, thanks to a swift, well-timed attack.

This escape is soon followed by another impressive action scene, with Lethbridge-Stewart getting into a fairly lengthy fist-fight with one of Reegan's gang. Naturally, the Brig wins, and then he's into the laboratory, guns still blazing, but blazing very precisely – he shoots Reegan's wrist, forcing him to drop his gun, and for the second time this story, the Doctor is rescued thanks to the Brigadier arriving in good time and shooting stuff[7].

It's not just square-jawed heroism we get from the Brig. Despite the excellent and pricey action set pieces earlier in the story, someone seems to have written a note to the writers during episode 7, asking them to tone it down a bit. And so, after the Brigadier makes his escape to UNIT HQ, he finds there are only one or two men there and no transport: everyone and everything's at Space Centre. Sergeant Benton suggests using the Doctor's car; the reaction shot of Nicholas Courtney's expression is priceless. And it also demonstrates that one doesn't need to turn the Brigadier into an idiot in order to have him provide effective comedy relief. It's also rather nice seeing the final third of the story's power trio get a shot behind the wheel of Bessie, though I doubt the Doctor would approve of seeing her loaded up with UNIT soldiers.

In terms of the trio, the Brigadier plays two roles. First, the superego (that's the Spock role) which, while usually in this context used to represent intellect, was also used by Freud to represent the

---

[7] Episode seven.

rules or social conventions. Of the three, the Brigadier is most at ease with, and inclined to follow, the normal rules of society. We see this especially in his interactions with General Carrington, a man the Brigadier clearly disagrees with quite strongly, but will not actively oppose because he is his superior officer, and will only speak out against by couching his language in terms the army deems an acceptable way to speak to a superior officer.

The Brigadier will also switch to the role of the id, representing emotion and instinct. He lacks the scientific training of the Doctor and Liz, and will act and make judgements based on his feelings. We see in the latter half of the story, when his leads have dried up, that he doesn't trust Carrington, and admits this mistrust is based purely on his gut instinct. More importantly, the first time we see him in this story, he's in the Space Centre, his attitude regarding the return of Mars Probe 7 in marked contrast to the civilian scientists running the project. While they remain calm and detached, the Brigadier shows emotion. The first time he speaks, it's to insist the astronaut check that the craft he's approaching is definitely Mars Probe 7[8]. It's only a hint of paranoia, of fear, but one that's allowed to peek out from the Brigadier's psyche, and in Carrington, we see what happens when such feelings are given free rein.

On the other side, when the Brigadier plays the part of the superego, the Doctor takes on the role of the id. He will reject authority, and rules, and even a timely rescue will be met with nothing more than an irritated 'what kept you?'[9] We see this role

---

[8] Episode one.
[9] Episode seven.

being played as the Doctor bursts into Space Centre at the beginning of the story, his red-lined cloak the only flash of colour amidst a sea of greys and silver. He's rude to everyone he speaks to, appalled at the very idea of carrying a pass, and, naturally, he is met with brusqueness by Space Centre staff. The Brigadier, as the superego, is the one who smoothes things over, reminding the Doctor that he might get what he wants rather more quickly if he followed human conventions, and stopped being quite so rude to everyone, especially the man in charge[10].

Where they switch round, and the Doctor becomes the superego, is when they fall into their roles as soldier and scientist. The Doctor relies on his intellect to solve problems, and trusts first to reason and logic; while the Brigadier will not make violence his first option, it will always be one that he'll consider. We see the most dramatic divergence between the two at the beginning of the story, where the Doctor is still angry about the Brigadier's murder of the Silurians[11]. There the Doctor favoured a peaceful, negotiated solution, one that would have taken time, trust, and patience to succeed, while the Brigadier – following orders, but orders he agreed with – brought about a destructive end to the conflict, motivated by fear. Liz Shaw provides the bridge between the two points of view. She doesn't agree with the Brigadier's destructive, fearful choice, but nor can she utterly condemn it as the Doctor does. She understands his fear, though she doesn't endorse it. The Doctor is simply horrified at the needless waste of life. (This isn't his world, after all, it's just another ridiculous conflict to him. But for the races living on Earth, who would have to live with the

---

[10] Episode one.
[11] In the previous story, *The Silurians*.

consequences, it's never as simple as laying down one's arms and sitting at the negotiating table until an agreement is hammered out. It should be – the alternative should horrify us so much that it should be – but it isn't. There are nuances to every conflict that can never be fully understood by the supposedly objective outsider. The anger, the mistrust, the fear, what each side sees as just and fair, and what is seen as petty, or vengeful – these things cannot simply evaporate, and to disregard them, to insist that they don't matter is foolish and naïve.)

In his third incarnation, Jon Pertwee's Doctor falls into a rather more traditional hero mould than his previous two personas, and in *Ambassadors*, his hero moment comes when Cornish finds he has a rocket to rescue the astronauts trapped in orbit, but no-one to pilot it. In a wonderfully underplayed moment, the Doctor steps forward, literally, and says he'll take the rocket up himself. Cornish is incredulous, of course, but we know the Doctor can do it. Even if he can't control the TARDIS all that well, as viewers we're well aware of his genius, and we saw him fly a rocket all the way to the Moon only a year ago in Troughton's story *The Seeds of Death* (1969).

Cornish, to his credit, hears the Doctor out, even though he calls the British rockets 'primitive' and boasts of being able to cope with more G-force than most people[12]. He agrees to let the Doctor take the astronaut tests, and when he reads the Doctor's medical report, Cornish describes it as 'incredible'. We never find out exactly what impresses Cornish so much, as the Doctor cuts him off, embarrassed. (We can guess what it says: Time Lord physiology

---

[12] Episode four.

has been shown, even ignoring regeneration, to be much stronger and hardier than human.)

In his most heroic moments of the episode, the Doctor blasts off into space, heading up to the Mars Probe 7 capsule alone, to rescue the three astronauts still in orbit whose life support is running out. (It's hard to imagine the first Doctor taking such an action hero role, though he would undoubtedly have a few sharp words for anyone who suggested he wasn't up to the job. The second Doctor we know from *The Seeds of Death* could do it, but it would be a jaunt for him, not a heroic rescue; the tension and tone of the piece would be entirely different.) He's also quite unfazed by the various attempts to kill him, and, falling back into the more conventional hero mode, dismisses his saboteurs with an unimpressed 'they're very persistent, aren't they?'

Despite the aura of heroism as he sets off in Recovery 7, the Doctor swiftly reverts to his core objectionable, rebellious persona, suspicious of any authority, even if it's mission control. He's bored with all the checks the capsule has to go through, and very keen that everyone else knows it, and wants them to hurry up. He irritably nitpicks at Cornish's words. 'I take it you mean half an hour,' he says tetchily as Cornish informs in that they're at 'zero minus 30, 3–0, minutes' till the launch,[13] And when Cornish asks if he has 'visual contact' with Mars Probe 7, the Doctor's reply is 'If you mean can I see it, the answer's "No".'[14]

His superior experience with spacecraft, and his scientific intelligence, is shown to good effect during this rescue mission

---

[13] Episode five.
[14] Episode five.

when, thanks to sabotage, the rocket is going too fast. He convinces Cornish to jettison stage one early in order to reduce speed so he'll make an Earth orbit, and won't be pushed into orbit around the Sun[15]. His descent back to Earth is also 'perfect' according to Cornish[16], though the Doctor remains pedantically averse to the jargon associated with space flight.

The Doctor may mock the procedures but he does respect them, to the extent that he complies with them in the absence of a pressing reason not to. The Doctor has no compunction about breaking rules or attacking red tape, but he does so with purpose. He isn't rebellious for the sake of being rebellious. He follows flight procedure, and he patiently waits for the decontamination procedure to be complete, despite voicing his irritation at both. Amusingly, he's equally irate when someone else[17] tells him to hurry it up.

As in the previous story, *The Silurians*, the Doctor finds himself negotiating on behalf of humanity. I say 'finds himself', but that's not quite right: he **appoints** himself humanity's ambassador, in a move that's highly presumptuous and shows a rather paternalistic view towards the human race. While I object to his assumption that he can speak for an entire race that's not even his own, it's hard to fault his motives or aims. The Doctor wants peace, and he wants to save lives. His vast experience of the cosmos also means he's free of fear of an alien being simply because it is different. He's able to

---

[15] While this episode was being filmed, the British launch system the Black Arrow was in use, and used a three-stage system to get into orbit, as is the launch system used in *Ambassadors*.

[16] Episode six.

[17] Reegan, in Episode seven.

trust easily, and to trust his own intuition regarding aliens' stated intentions. The trust is met with trust in return. The Silurians believed him, to their destruction, and so do these aliens, who the Doctor is able to persuade to let him go, to try and find their Ambassadors and return them to their people. In echoing the previous story, and showing humanity making a wiser decision, the story suggests we've earned a little redemption.

At one point Carrington wants to know if the rocket is capable of carrying a nuclear weapon. The Doctor's response: 'Since we don't know what's up there, wouldn't it be more intelligent to carry a man rather than a bomb?'[18] It's a lovely summing-up of the Doctor's attitude towards exploration and discovery, and a succinct condemnation of humanity when we let our fear overcome our thirst for knowledge.

Making the central trio of characters more compelling is, as mentioned earlier, a Doctor who is in a particularly vulnerable position. He's not just trapped on Earth, but his mind has been interfered with by the Time Lords, and parts of his knowledge have been blocked off. His frustration with the situation is clear when he recognises the sound the aliens send, but he can't remember from where, or what it means.

His knowledge might be affected, but his intelligence certainly isn't. There's a wonderful demonstration of the Doctor's eccentric brilliance in the wake of Recovery 7 being stolen from UNIT. Here, the Doctor blocks the road with Bessie, pretends to be a doddering old fellow, and traps them with Bessie's anti-theft device. It's a

---

[18] Episode five.

smashing example of the limits of military might and brute force versus sufficient guile and scientific cunning.

And, while his appearance may have changed, and his outer character is rather more brusque and unfriendly compared to his predecessor, we most clearly see he's the same person in moments of crisis. If he's bored, he becomes distracted by the next exciting or shiny thing that happens, and Liz gets left in the laboratory (since she's by far the more conscientious of the two); but when lives are in immediate danger, the Doctor suddenly finds his focus. When the Brigadier appears to send a note to the Doctor and Liz requesting their help in examining some bodies killed by radiation, the Doctor declines to leave, despite previously getting out of the lab on any excuse, because there's now a space capsule to get ready to rescue the orbiting astronauts.

Despite the fact the Doctor's first priority tends to be to save lives, he's not moved by threats. When Reegan telephones him to tell him that if he doesn't 'stop interfering' then Liz will be killed, he doesn't responds with fear, anger, or threats of his own. He is coolly defiant, not reacting while on the telephone, and immediately getting back to work once the call has ended[19]. Fear is entirely absent from the Doctor's feelings or motivations throughout the story, and in *Ambassadors*, it's fear, more than anyone or anything else, that's the enemy.

Liz Shaw, the third side of the season seven trio, is always Freud's ego, the resolving force between the other two. She shares the Doctor's scientific expertise, but is immersed in human structures and hierarchies, and has a respect for them not easily overruled.

---

[19] Episode four.

She relies on her reason and intelligence to solve problems, but though she has a great deal of self-control she is affected by emotions. In response to the attack on the Silurians, Liz didn't agree with the Brigadier's action, but nor could she find it within herself to condemn it with the same ferocity as the Doctor. Here, in *Ambassadors*, Liz is pushed far further out of her comfort zone than either the Doctor or the Brigadier: she's kidnapped and forced to help keep the Ambassadors alive with the use of radioactive isotopes that have the potential to kill her if she makes a mistake. This added stress and the removal of any sort of support network allows a better look into Liz Shaw's character and, in particular, how she deals with fear.

When a gun is turned on her at the beginning of episode two, Liz Shaw responds to Taltalian's threats with mockery. She wants to be entirely unintimidated by the threat of violence, but we see how frightened she is when Taltalian grabs her, puts the gun to her temple, and can no longer see her face. When she's released, she needs to time to recover, but her first concern is how the Doctor managed to hide the tape Taltalian was after.

While Liz doesn't get a lot of onscreen time in the first hour or so, as we're heading out of episode three she splits off from the Doctor as she goes solo to examine the bodies found by the Brigadier. She goes to the scene of the crime alone, driving the Doctor's beloved car Bessie – a testament to the Doctor's trust in her.

She never makes it to the bodies – the message is a trick – and instead gets to star in a turn of events worthy of Emma Peel, as she becomes involved in a rather rare **Doctor Who** event: a car chase. It's a well done action sequence in a story that's full of them, and it's especially wonderful to see Liz at the heart of it. She acquits herself admirably, though the modern car pursing her eventually forces her to stop. That's not the end of things, however, and she makes a run for it, outpacing her pursuers across an open field, and making it to a river. She races across a weir at a pace that I don't feel is done justice with the direction – it's a very narrow surface, it's wet and slippery, and there's only a barrier on one side. What she is doing is extremely dangerous, but watching it doesn't quite have the edge of the seat 'Oh my God, she's going to fall in' terror it should have. As her pursuers catch up with her, she punches one back – he falls, almost into the river, and is left clinging onto the side of the weir. Liz then tries to escape her other attacker by jumping over the barrier and into the fast flowing river below. She fails, but the attempt was nonetheless awesome[20].

She is no more impressed by these men and their violence than she was by Taltalian. In the face of violence and threats, she remains fiercely obstinate. The first chance she gets, she – very sensibly – grabs her coat and makes for the door. It's locked, so she turns on the scientist helping the thugs, Doctor Lennox, and, after ascertaining that he has a key, works on him to convince him to give it to her. She appeals to his pride, his past as a respected scientist, and it doesn't take much prodding for her to convince him to give her what she wants. Liz is compassionate, but practical – she asks Lennox to go with her, but when he's reluctant, doesn't waste any time trying to persuade him, and makes a run for it alone. Her energetic run through the dirt roads of the country brings her to an actual road with actual cars. Unfortunately, the

---

[20] Episode three.

first car she flags down is driven by the treacherous Dr Taltalian, who comes armed with a gun, and takes her back to Reegan and Lennox's laboratory hideout.

One the one hand, yes, this is padding since the plot doesn't advance, but more importantly it's excellent characterisation of Liz, where we see her under serious pressure, outside a purely scientific context, and with no friends or allies. Even when recaptured, she remains defiant, and she doesn't give Lennox away. She's also undeterred from her determination to escape. 'If at first you don't succeed... ' she says, eyes bright, and with a fierce smile[21].

After being recaptured, Liz Shaw resumes pressing Lennox, gathering from him as much information as she can about what they're doing and who they're working for. While she realises she'll find it exceptionally difficult to escape again, she turns her focus towards converting Lennox to her cause. She takes full advantage of Reegan's willingness to boast about his attack with the Ambassadors, questioning him on exactly what happened. Here, we see her softer side for a few brief moments, as she's clearly worried about her friends. She immediately takes advantage of her new knowledge to apply more pressure to Lennox and his conscience, forcing him to face the fact that he is working for a murderer. Lennox tries to distance himself from Reegan and his gang, but Liz is unrelenting, insisting he's 'just as guilty as if [he'd] killed those people [himself].' She won't let him disassociate himself from them, won't let him claim he's helpless or trapped. Instead, she gives him a way out, an excuse to leave the lab, and a

---

[21] Episode four.

way to be safe – to go to UNIT and speak to Lethbridge-Stewart – and insists over his protests again, and again, that he has to get a message to UNIT, that he has to **try**. It's a battle of wills and one where Liz is clearly going to be the victor.

When Lennox finally attempts to leave the lab, Liz doesn't leave him on his own. Seeing he's in trouble even just confronting Reegan's henchman, she steps up to lie about the health of the Ambassadors, feigning openness regarding the radiation readings while relying on the henchman's ignorance to not understand the equipment. Once they're committed, Lennox insists on being let out as the henchman is there to guard Liz, not him. There's a small smile from Liz as he does this, and it's a tiny bit of heroism, all the more satisfying because it comes from a man who's so clearly terrified and has lost his way. When he finally does make it out the door, there's a quick, brilliant smile from Liz, taking a moment to enjoy her success.

Liz's indefatigable attitude is not brittle, however; she will bend, if that's what she believes she needs to do to survive. When questioned by Reegan, after Lennox's escape, she relents when he presses the barrel of a gun to her neck. He's already murdered several people, of which she's well aware, and so she tells him where Lennox has gone. The information she gives isn't valuable: Reegan is only looking for a confirmation of what he's already guessed, and it's the most obvious place Lennox could have gone, and the most dangerous for Reegan – whatever Liz said, UNIT is where Reegan's attention would focus first.

Despite giving up the information, she remains unimpressed by further threats, and her response to the thug telling her 'Don't try anything' is probably Liz Shaw's greatest line: 'Don't worry, I won't hurt you.'[22]

The closest we come to see Liz losing her steady self-control is when one of the Ambassadors finally reveals his face[23]. She's clearly afraid, but her response to that fear is to seek more information about what she's seen, about the source of her fear. Knowledge, more than anything else, is her surest defence. And, once she's rescued, there's a suggestion that at least some of her defiance was bravura when, after the Brigadier arrives, all she says is, 'Just get me out of here.'[24] It's a superbly played moment, where Liz, feeling safe at last, allows her defences down just a little, and we can see the strain the ordeal has taken on her.

---

[22] Episode five.
[23] Episode six.
[24] Episode seven.

HOLMES AND WATSON

The Doctor and the Brigadier have a friendship that last decades, or centuries, depending on how you look at it, and in that time the dynamic between them goes through various permutations, but none feels quite so complex as the relationship we see in play in season seven. In many ways, it's like the early days of Sherlock Holmes and Dr Watson[25], where there is clearly a mutual respect between the characters but they've not yet closed the distance from colleagues to friends. It gives an added layer of satisfyingly complex tension to their interactions.

The dynamic is set up quite succinctly in the first half of episode one, when the Doctor watches the television broadcast of the Recovery 7 mission. 'And the Brigadier thinks it's his business,' he says, waspishly, after spotting the military presence in mission control. 'I suppose he's got to do something to occupy his mind now that he's blown up the Silurians.' The Doctor's rudeness might extend to the Brigadier, but the Brigadier, being fully aware of the Doctor's brilliance and how he's brought it to bear against alien attacks on the Earth, has considerably more patience for the Doctor's snark than any other human. And the will to intercede on his behalf, to press him towards politeness, and to ask others for patience with his tetchy colleague. Importantly, the Doctor is prepared to listen to the Brigadier on these points: when he takes the Doctor aside after he barges into Space Centre, and reminds him that there is a hierarchy here, and that Cornish is in charge, the Doctor calms down instantly, and takes the point. This Doctor,

---

[25] See, for instance, Conan Doyle, Arthur, *A Study in Scarlet* (1887) and *The Sign of Four* (1890).

more than any other, is aware of human hierarchies, having been forced to live within them for an extended, continuous amount of time. At the Brigadier's urging, he attempts politeness and persuasiveness, arguing that the message must be decoded for the safety of the astronauts, who are Cornish's primary concern. 'I suppose we must try everything,' says Cornish, conceding both to practicality – whatever they can do to help the astronauts, they must – and the Doctor's argument, whilst subtly, and so Britishly, rebuking the Doctor for his rudeness[26].

The Brigadier isn't above returning a little snark of his own, and who can blame him? This Doctor is clearly not an easy person to get along with. 'We'll see you at the Space Centre... if you make it,' says the Brigadier after they go out to retrieve Recovery 7[27]. He's aiming this little dig at the suitability of the Doctor's Edwardian roadster, Bessie. It's a particularly interesting moment because he makes almost exactly the same comment in the season 10 story *The Time Monster* (1972), but there is a very different feel to it[28]. In *Ambassadors* Bessie starts, stalls, and stops while the Recovery 7 convoy is well on its way. The Doctor trails well behind the Brigadier and his soldiers and, even though this means he is in a position to use a spot of cunning to steal back Recovery 7, it's clear that the Brigadier had a point. In *The Time Monster*, however, we are invited to laugh at the silly Brigadier, because the Doctor has souped up Bessie, who's now absurdly fast, and poor old Brig is left behind. The power balance in the relationship will shift dramatically

---

[26] Episode one.
[27] Episode two.
[28] 'See you there. Try not to be far behind.' (*The Time Monster* Episode three).

after season seven, and much to the detriment of the Brigadier's character.

Towards the end of the story, Cornish makes a damning attack on the failures of the military, and the Brigadier's investigation: 'The astronauts are still missing, Miss Shaw kidnapped, Doctor Taltalian killed, and now this man Lennox murdered.'[29] The Brigadier, to his credit, responds with what his people have discovered. They know the bodies found weren't foreign agents, but petty criminals; that the explosive that killed Taltalian was brand new and hadn't yet been issued to the army, lending credence to the Doctor's theory. In a truly Holmesian move, the Brigadier has had the mud on Lennox's boots analysed, and his forensic team found an insecticide in it, so they're tracking down where that chemical's been in use. He's also found out where the isotope that killed Lennox came from. It's an impressive investigation, and an excellent moment from the Brigadier as, after accosting him for his lack of success, Cornish is forced to admit he's 'been very thorough.' Unfortunately, for all his diligence, the clues have led nowhere. In another moment of decent deductive reasoning from the Brigadier, he voices his suspicion that Carrington knows much more than he's saying, sensitive to the man's seeming paranoia regarding the alien ship, and remembering that Carrington used to be an astronaut, and visited Mars himself on Mars Probe 6. Like Watson, he's an intelligent man, but finds himself at a dead end, as he lacks the brilliance of a Liz, a Doctor or a Holmes to spark an insight that would unravel the mystery. Meanwhile, the Doctor's in his element as a Holmesian investigator, and able to point to the correct

---

[29] Episode six.

solutions that fit all the evidence, however unlikely. He's the one who works out that the three astronauts are still in orbit, and the three who've come to Earth are in fact aliens.

The most wonderful scene between the Doctor and the Brigadier, illustrating their relationship at this point, occurs when the Doctor's about to launch into the rocket. The Brigadier has decided to see him off, and the Doctor's a little surprised at the gesture. They exchange a few words of polite conversation before the Brigadier shakes his hand, wishes him luck, and they say their goodbyes. It's a compelling scene because we see so clearly how the two characters are still fundamentally uncomfortable with one another, while still sharing a mutual respect, one that edges ever closer to genuine friendship, but isn't quite there yet. There's a stiffness, a formality, to their interaction here that adds a layer to their relationship that would become decidedly less complicated in later years.

The Holmes and Watson vibe is helped enormously by the fact that a good chunk of *Ambassadors* is set up as a mystery, and a space mystery too – surely the very best kind of mystery. The story opens by setting up the first question: what happened to Mars Probe 7? And it quickly follows with a series of other, related mysteries. A message is transmitted from Recovery 7, twice, and, wonderfully, when there is a third message, the Doctor can tell the difference between one horrible sound and another. (So can the viewer if they rewind – they are very different.) And another delicious layer is added to the mystery: someone has replied to the first message, but who? And why? (And just in case we didn't pick up on how the mystery is deepened, Michael Wisher is there to tell us.)

STEED AND PEEL

Liz Shaw and the Doctor blend into a wonderfully effective team during their time together, one that feels rather like John Steed and Emma Peel[30], if Steed and Peel were less secret agents and more scientific geniuses. Every time I see Liz and the Doctor together, it hurts a little that I know they only have the one year, and not nearly enough scenes together.

In the early episodes of *Ambassadors*, there's a clear contrast drawn between their work methods. While the Doctor is keen on patience, he's less able to get on with any work that actually requires sustained concentration and effort, areas where Liz Shaw is show to excel. With the taped message, Liz is the one who works on the decoding, while the Doctor is off with the Brigadier playing at interrogator. And when the decoding fails, Liz is the one who theorises why. To test the theory, and illustrating how beautifully their methods can dovetail, when Liz suggests running a test program to check if there's a computer fault that messed up the decoding, the Doctor tells her to just ask it what two plus two is. The computer says five. The Doctor dismisses the computer as untrustworthy, but Liz, with a better understanding of computers, dismisses that suggestion, and insists Taltalian must have sabotaged it.

With the computer fixed, it's back to Liz doing the actual decoding work, while the Doctor goes off on a jaunt with the Brigadier and soldiers to find Recovery 7. There's no particularly good reason for him to be there, but the Doctor prefers to be at the centre of

---

[30] In **The Avengers** (1961-69). Diana Rigg's Mrs Peel was a central character alongside Patrick Macnee's Steed from 1965-68.

where the action is, improvising solutions on the spur of the moment, rather than actually getting on with any proper work. He only shows further interest in the message once Liz informs him that she's made progress on decoding it, enough for the Doctor to be certain that the origin of the message is extraterrestrial – an assessment Liz lacks the experience and knowledge to make, but he could never have made without Liz actually getting the decoding work done.

The Doctor doesn't really trust many humans. It's bad enough seeing him be disruptive and rude when he barges into Space Centre, but the most wince-inducing moment comes after Recovery 7 is cut open. Cornish pops his head inside, and is shocked to find it empty. 'What?' says the Doctor. 'Let me see!'[31] Yes, Doctor, because Ralph Cornish might not have checked... where? In all the corners? On the ceiling? Of course he could be looking for clues to what has happened to the astronauts, but the way it's played seems to suggest he just can't take Cornish's word on the capsule being empty. (Maybe he has a point – Cornish doesn't seem to spot the very obvious, very 1970s, tape recorder that's playing the repeated message purporting to be from the Recovery 7 astronauts.)

Notably, however, the Doctor trusts he's seen all he needs to see with that one quick look inside the capsule – he is brilliant, after all, so what could he possibly have missed? Liz Shaw, always the more diligent of the two, does bother with a second look and finds a crucial clue none of the others spotted: the Geiger counter indicates that the interior of the capsule has somehow become

---

[31] *The Ambassadors of Death* Episode three.

highly radioactive, sufficiently so to kill any human being who spent time in the capsule.

The Doctor checks Taltalian isn't armed by poking a pencil in the man's back and enquiring, a move quite worthy of Steed and his umbrella. Still suspicious of the other scientist, the Doctor openly tells him what he thinks, and offers him the choice of 'a ruthless investigation by the Brigadier, or a few quiet words with me, and [his] name kept out of things.'[32] The value of reputation, and discretion: there's a sort of devious honesty to the Doctor's way of doing things and, again, one could easily envision Steed in his place here.

There's something quite wonderful too, about the way the Doctor and Liz fall into their method of teamwork as soon as they're reunited, and the Doctor is conscious. The Doctor spots the Ambassadors, and is fascinated while Liz fills him in on what she knows about them, and he updates her on his contact with their captain. Reegan, still there, still armed, is rendered irrelevant. The instant Reegan's out the door, there's another demonstration of the Doctor and Liz's easy understanding of one another, as they silently communicate by gesture. While Liz has exhausted her options for conventional escape and concentrated on information-gathering, the Doctor confidently comes up with an unorthodox plan to get away within minutes of regaining consciousness. We see them working in tandem on the communications device, cleverly remaking it to instead broadcast an SOS so UNIT will be alerted to their position. Once they're finished, there's another visual parallel drawn between them: they both sit in the laboratory,

---

[32] Episode four.

arms folded and legs crossed as they glare daggers at the poor henchman who's been left to guard them.

The relationship between Liz Shaw and the Doctor tends to be overshadowed by the much longer-lasting, and more openly affectionate, partnership between the Doctor and Jo Grant, but despite their short tenure together, and Liz's reticence to believe the Doctor's more extraordinary claims, there still exists a deep affection between them. In *Ambassadors* this is most clearly seen in the moment they're reunited in the penultimate episode, having been parted ever since Liz was kidnapped. The Doctor comes round from unconsciousness, lying on the floor, while Liz kneels by his head. There's warmth and relief in both their voices that the other is all right, but the most telling gesture comes from the Doctor, as he reaches up and gently brushes the hair back from Liz's face, and holds it there. It's a tender gesture, and in a series where it was considered too risqué to show the Brigadier's wife asleep in their bed, a terribly intimate one too.

WEALTH, SECURITY, AND KNOWLEDGE

Looking beyond the regulars, we find there are three primary factors that control and motivate the supporting cast for the story: desire for wealth, desire for security, and desire for knowledge. The primary conflict is between the desire for knowledge, as represented by the scientists, and the desire for security, as represented by the military; but we also have the Brigadier as the thoughtful soldier; and see knowledge corrupted by greed in our two fallen scientists, Taltalian and Lennox, and wealth used to try and buy security.

The characters that represent these three conflicting desires, or temptations perhaps, are Reegan, Carrington, and Cornish.

Turning to Reegan first, we find an immensely satisfying villain. He's amoral, very practical, and he has an excellent work ethic. If you're looking to hire yourself a thug, this is the kind of man you want. Reegan is the villain motivated by money. He does the job he's paid for, so long as he gets his money, and he's happy. In his fear, this is the man Carrington has turned to. He'll trust Reegan, who is only interested in money, but not the Brigadier, because he works for an international organisation.

Reegan's most coolly villainous moment happens when he hands over a suitcase bomb to Taltalian. '15 minutes,' he says to Taltalian, setting the timer. 'That's how long you have to get away once you activate it.' Then as Taltalian turns away to put on his coat, Reegan, smooth as you like, opens the suitcase, flicks the timer back, and closes it again, all before Taltalian turns round to be handed the suitcase. It's all done so casually, and so neatly timed, as to demonstrate better than anything else in the story Reegan's character. Though he can't resist the parting shot, with a double meaning that anyone who realises they're in a spy movie should beware of: 'Do as you're told and your troubles will be over.'[33]

The man may enjoy his Bond-esque double-entendres, but when it comes to killing people, or even just plain old violence, it's clear Reegan's no sadist. He just does whatever's practical, or what he's being paid for. What causes him to be positively gleeful are the imagined possibilities once he's used the Ambassadors in a successful raid; he's thrilled at how quickly and easily they can kill, how useless conventional weapons are against them, and boasts of what he's made them to Liz and Lennox. The first thing he thinks of when he believes he can use them to do anything is 'Walk into Fort Knox'[34]. Liz is suitably unimpressed that his wildest dream is to steal a lot of gold.

Reegan is also a very hands-on sort of villain. No leaving the work to minions for him – he's happy to impersonate soldiers or scientists, set bombs, dump bodies, and kill with bullets, radiation, or sabotage to the fuel injection system. It's all just a job to him, and if he's getting paid, he's got no problem getting on with it. It's nice to see a villain with such a solid work ethic. One imagines that if he only applied this diligence to a more legitimate activity, he'd actually do rather well for himself.

When he captures the Doctor, Reegan is much less interested in killing him than he is in using him and his scientific expertise for his own material gain. He's happy to steal or buy whatever equipment the Doctor needs in order to make a more effective

---

[33] Episode four.
[34] Episode five.

45

communications advice, one that goes beyond giving the Ambassadors simple orders. Presumably he wants it mostly so he can carry out more complicated robberies.

By the end, Reegan's in a smart suit, handkerchief in breast pocket and all, and in ever such a civilised way he's going through his plans for his next robbery with the Doctor. He seems to be of the view that if he's just persistent enough, he can surely convince the Doctor to join him. And, in a move worthy of the sheer practicality Reegan's shown throughout the story, he's the one who, after being captured and shot, suggests the plan to get back into the Space Centre: use the Ambassadors. 'You won't forget I thought of it?' he says, his final line. This is a man who knows when to quit. The desire for money motivates him, it gives him a reason to commit numerous criminal acts, but it never overcomes him. Carrington tells him he's 'not paid to think,' but Reegan never stops[35]. He's an incredibly sensible sort of villain, always looking for an angle to advance his own interests, but never pushing anything to extremes, never so greedy as to destroy himself. In a canon of power-mad villains where planetary, if not universal, Armageddon is a regular possibility, it's refreshing to have an antagonist who's both competent and small-scale. He's realistic in a way few **Who** villains tend to be, one who could easily walk off this set, and into **The Sweeney** (1975-78) without changing a thing about his character.

The Space Centre Controller, Ralph Cornish, has quite different motivations. Throughout *Ambassadors*, his primary concern is the safe return of his astronauts, but he's also part of the scientific

---

[35] Episode seven.

agenda: one of those characters who value knowledge first. In the absence of the Doctor and Liz Shaw, he's the one who steps up to act as the sensible, logical voice against the fear-driven irrationality of General Carrington.

His restrained performance is just the sort of thing I think you'd want to hear if you were trapped in a tin bucket millions of miles away from home. He also remains resolutely unflappable throughout the story, staying calm and focused through sabotage, kidnap, murder, aliens, and military takeovers. During the initial linkup between Recovery 7 and Mars Probe 7 – the final moments of a mission that has taken eight months to get to this point – the only sign of strain we see from Cornish is a single finger rubbing his brow. His expression remains neutral, and voice detached, even as the rescue astronaut reports hearing noises on the other side of the airlock. In contrast, we see the Brigadier already smiling, already ready to celebrate. We hear Cornish at his most emotive when he's asking about the astronauts, **his** astronauts, and he's clearly very protective about them.

On the larger scale, Cornish's sympathies lie firmly on the side of peaceful exploration, and the expansion of humanity's knowledge of the universe. When the Doctor and Liz Shaw are absent from Space Centre, he's the one who demands to know if the Brigadier supports Carrington's plan 'to attack blindly.'[36] Interestingly, those on the scientific side of this divide aren't pacifists, or even anti-war, but they are, at the very least, believers in the theory of the just war. Cornish isn't necessarily against attacking, but he is against attacking the unknown. If there is to be an attack, let it be a

---

[36] Episode six.

reasoned one, with just cause, after all other alternatives have been explored and exhausted.

After the Doctor's gone through the appropriate tests, Cornish, ever practical, in many ways the ideal scientist, considers the Doctor 'perfectly capable of making the trip' up in the Recovery capsule, despite their initial antagonistic meeting, and the fact that the Doctor isn't a part of the British astronaut programme.

In a last-ditch attempt to stop the rescue mission, Carrington goes to the Space Centre himself and 'absolutely forbids' the launch. Cornish is coolly unimpressed, and instantly dismisses him because he doesn't have 'the authority to forbid it.'[37] This is a civilian operation, and Cornish is not a man to be intimidated. He's also a man of principle: faced with Carrington making what he considers a disastrous broadcast, Cornish doesn't back down, or stop trying to get Carrington to see reason until he's forcibly removed by Carrington's soldiers. It's emblematic of the fundamental conflict we see at work in *Ambassadors*, one which has plagued humanity since our earliest days of civilisation, and no doubt before recorded history too. We see two of our primal impulses at war: our fear, and our curiosity. Our urge to strike out and attack what might hurt us, versus our desire to reach out and try to understand the unknown.

General Carrington is a magnificent character, and wonderfully played by John Abineri. **Doctor Who** likes to deal in monsters, and while those monsters are often metaphors for the particular fears and anxieties of the society from the time the story was made, they remain monsters. They are, if not evil, at least unrepentantly

---

[37] Episode five.

destructive, and must be stopped. When we get a villain, often more nuanced in their plan or motivation, often terribly charismatic, we might enjoy the character, but in the end it's hard to dispute that they're wearing a black hat. Carrington is the rarest, and most thoughtful, type of **Doctor Who** antagonist: sympathetic. This is a flawed man, who had the potential to be great, but has allowed himself to become consumed by his fear.

Carrington is responsible for Space Security, and Cornish is responsible for the Space Centre and its operations, and both are fiercely protective of their fields of influence. Cornish, in particular, is cool and collected in the face of threats and bluster from Carrington. He won't be provoked or dissuaded. Faced with the unknown, we see the two sides in action. The Space Centre, and its peers, do all they can to gather information. The Americans are planning to send a satellite up to take a closer look, while a radio telescope has detected radio pulses from the alien ship of 'a frequency similar to those emitted by pulsars.'[38] In contrast, Carrington has a single plan, a single focus: destroy the alien ship.

We also see bureaucracy at work, further pushing Carrington down the road of self-destruction. There's the slow grind of the Security Council meeting in Geneva,[39] moving far too slowly for Carrington's liking. He returns to the Space Centre before it's even concluded, if anything even more belligerent than when he left. (If only this was a dictatorship, and he was in charge, surely that would be safest of all…) He wants every missile they have armed with an atomic

---

[38] Episode six.
[39] Presumably the United Nations, but as this is near-future setting, it could be a European initiative.

warhead and fired at the alien ship. Cornish considers this extreme, Carrington believes it's their 'moral duty'. It's the first time he uses this phrase, and it's one he clings to through the rest of the story. Destroying the aliens is the **moral** thing to do.

Cornish genuinely believes Carrington to be insane. 'Insanity' is a word flung about rather easily in this sort of pulpy science-fantasy world that **Doctor Who** normally inhabits. Every grandiose alien warlord on a power trip to conquer the universe is 'insane', but in season seven, the accusation of insanity feels heavier. Cornish, throughout the story, has been shown to be an exceptionally level-headed, reasonable, and open-minded individual. For him to judge a man insane is an assessment to be taken seriously, and he delivers it so mildly, with a touch light enough to feel like sadness at the state of Carrington.

Part of the brilliance of Carrington as a character is that he seems a rather self-effacing antagonist. When he's first introduced to the Doctor, Liz, and the Brigadier, he's amicable, and apologetic regarding what's happened. He admits to everything that he'd done so far – that they're aware of – and seems regretful for the trouble he's put them to. He apologises again when he interrupts the Doctor, and the Doctor responds that he can't get any work done if he's disturbed[40].

The first hints of the single-minded destructive focus that lies beneath comes when he attempts to plant evidence on several dead bodies that have been found. He claims that they're foreign agents, carrying a newspaper in a foreign language, clothes with labels in a foreign language. Which language? It doesn't matter. It's

---

[40] Episode three.

foreign, different: that's the important thing. The different, the unknown, it's all just one great bulbous mass to point at and blame for any problems, and it's something to be afraid of. The motive Carrington ascribes to these fictitious agents is that they want to use the irradiated astronauts as a weapon, neatly following the pattern of assuming his foes, even his fictitious foes, want to do to him what he would do to them, if he could.

'If that rocket goes up, it means disaster for the entire world,' says Carrington, and he believes it too[41]. In his own mind, he isn't even a hero: there's nothing grandiose about Carrington. He's played in a very unassuming manner, very gentle. He's simply doing what he believes to be right: not right for him, or his career or power or legacy; he's doing it to protect his planet. Years later, in *Battlefield* (1988), we get two lines from the Brigadier that are both rather brilliant, and sum up his character beautifully: 'I just do the best I can,' and 'Get off my world.'[42] How easily those same lines could apply to Carrington, and how right he could have been. After all, how many alien species have come to Earth in peace? Can we assume Carrington didn't know about the previous attempted invasions?

In fact, in the context of **Doctor Who** as a whole, can we reasonably consider Carrington to be utterly alienated from his reason? At this point, Earth as already been invaded several times by alien species more advanced than our own. UNIT was set up because of alien invasions[43]. And it's not just that there have been invasions: the

---

[41] Episode four.

[42] *Battlefield* Episode four.

[43] If we retcon things, we've also got Torchwood in the background, ready to defend the United Kingdom against any and all threats.

vast majority of species encountered in **Doctor Who** are actively hostile. If it had been the Daleks encountered by Carrington, or the Cybermen, surely his actions would then be justified? Isn't it just his bad luck that the aliens of this story happens to be peaceful? Wouldn't he be a hero any other week?

The answer to these questions will depend on how afraid you are of the unknown.

Carrington's conviction that he's right, and that the right thing to do is to start firing nuclear missiles at other intelligent beings, is the most terrifying thing about him. When he's confronted with obstacles, he blusters, and that's rather more reassuring, but for most of the story he remains relatively calm, cool and considered as he talks about attacking and destroying other beings as though it's as obvious as rain being wet. He is gripped by paranoia and fear, unable to show the reasoning behind either, oblivious to the irony that he must manufacture evidence in order to convince anyone else of the threat, and utterly certain he's doing the right thing.

As the opposition stacks up, Carrington becomes increasingly paranoid, his mind twisting round in tighter and tighter circles. He tries to put blame for the attacks, and the Doctor's own kidnapping, on the Doctor himself, but the Brigadier is having none of it. Carrington tries to ignite mistrust of the Doctor in Cornish and the Brigadier by questioning who he is, where he comes from, and how the Brigadier knows him. Even the Brigadier, at this point, can't really answer these questions, but these seeds of doubt find no fertile ground as the Doctor has already won the Brigadier's trust, though his actions.

The Doctor shows no surprise when Carrington reveals himself to be the man behind the entire operation, or that Carrington ordered him killed. Again, he uses the phrase 'moral duty'[44]. One might be able to understand why he feels morally obliged to attack a superior alien race, but his moral duty to kill the Doctor? Why? He doesn't know that the Doctor is an alien. Has his reason departed so completely that he believes if he simply keeps killing people somehow it will all work out? He apologises for what he intends to do, and he clearly takes no pleasure in it. If anything, he seems tired, worn out; the strain of being the mastermind behind an elaborate conspiracy must be taking its toll.

Carrington, in as close as he comes to real anger, rebukes Reegan for disobeying an order. Reegan 'thought it was for the best' - and by 'the best', Reegan means best for his illicit bank balance. He's not keen on getting rid of useful people. Reegan goes for a little reverse-psychology on Carrington, telling him he needs the Doctor to create a more complex communications device so the Ambassadors can carry out Carrington's orders – but, heh, kill the Doctor if that's what you want. Surprisingly (or perhaps not, given Carrington's fragile mental state), this works, and Carrington begins to see in the Doctor a potential ally, or perhaps someone to confess to. Carrington has been alone for months, and has trusted no-one - not even his ally in the ministry - with his full plan. Sir James Quinlan, Carrington admits, wasn't a part of Carrington's full conspiracy. He was in it, as Carrington puts it, for the 'political glory of being the first to arrange contact with an intelligent alien

---

[44] *The Ambassadors of Death* Episode six.

species.' There's an irony to all this confessing, in that Carrington is speaking to the Doctor, unaware of his alien origins.

During Carrington's confession to his full part in the conspiracy and his consistent insistence that the aliens must be killed, we discover the event that triggered it off: the aliens accidently killed one of his fellow astronauts. It was a simple mistake on the part of the aliens, a single moment of carelessness out of which this whole series of events unfurled.

Carrington doesn't just want to destroy the Ambassadors and their ship, he wants the public on his side. To this end, he summons the Ambassadors to Earth, has them kidnapped and then plans to show one to the world, igniting a wave of fear and panic with his rhetoric, without any proof to his claims. The journalist, John Wakefield, has noticed this might be a problem. 'Has it occurred to you, sir,' he asks, 'that this may create world panic?' Of course that's what Carrington wants. Frightened people are easier to control and quicker to turn towards violence, frightened people will listen to his direct, simple plan, and won't take the time to reflect on the fact the only evidence offered that the aliens are dangerous is that they are not human.

Indeed, the sole evidence of their hostile intent is manufactured by Carrington, but this doesn't seem to stop him from seeing it as further proof that they must be destroyed. When the Brigadier reports that 'Aliens have raided an isotope factory, several deaths', Carrington immediately points to this as evidence of their hostility, and that their invasion has begun - and he seems actually to believe it, and not to be cognisant of the fact that he ordered the attack. When the Brigadier points out that there were men helping them,

Carrington calls them 'traitors, collaborators, like your friend the Doctor.' And soon, the Brigadier joins the list of traitors and is arrested. The spiral of paranoia widens, dragging everything down with it. Wonderfully, even in the face of Carrington arresting the Brigadier, Cornish remains unintimidated, and truthful. He attempts, in full view of Carrington, to contact the Ministry, and he asserts, once again, his authority over Space Centre.

Carrington's actions are propelled and justified by fear and paranoia, and they have consumed his reason to such an extent that he's able to know and believe two contrary pieces of information at once: he's ordering the aliens to attack, and the aliens are hostile, because they are attacking. Of course he can't let anyone else in on the plan; no-one else can be trusted. He's the only one who can save the world; only he understands the threat. And the tragedy is, he genuinely believes it. Imagine believing that you have a plan to save the world, and no-one else can possibly be told what it is. Carrington answering the Doctor and Liz's questions makes a lot of sense in this context: they can't hurt him, they're his prisoners, and he been carrying this massive burden around with him for months, and maybe, just maybe they'll understand, they'll know why he has to do it. By the standards of the trope of the villain revealing their plans to the presumed-doomed hero, this one makes a lot of psychological sense.

In the final moments of the story, UNIT rushes in, and stops Carrington's broadcast to the world. Carrington pleads with the Brigadier: 'I must make this broadcast – it's a matter of world survival.' He seems utterly perplexed at the idea the Brigadier is placing him under arrest. 'The sergeant will look after you,' the Brig tells him, softly. Carrington's final words are for the Doctor. 'I had to do what I did. It was my moral duty; you do understand, don't you?' There's no anger in the Doctor's response, as he says, 'Yes, General, I understand.'[45] The man has lost his way, and in the face of the violence, death, and fear he's wrought, the Doctor responds with compassion. He is an alien, protected only because he looks human, but the Doctor in his greatest moments shows the greatest humanity. And here, he chooses to end the fear and violence Carrington sought to inflict, by treating the man with dignity and consideration.

Rounding out the cast are Taltalian, a scientist who lets his fear get the better of him and is blown up by his own bomb; Lennox, another corrupted scientist, 'grossly underpaid'; and Sir James Quinlan, a civil servant, who'll be discussed in more detail later.

Which just leaves one question...

---

[45] Episode seven.

WHERE ARE ALL THE WOMEN?

The Ambassadors of Death suffers as most **Doctor Who** stories did before the late 1980s, and indeed has done on occasions since: there's a dearth of female characters. Before the '80s if there are even three speaking roles given to women in a story, then it gets a small cheer from me. *Ambassadors* just scrapes in. Across the seven episodes, we have three female speaking roles – Liz Shaw and Miss Rutherford, and an unnamed scientist (though the latter two seem more like the same role, but for some reason they didn't re-hire the same actor) – while there are 32 male ones. There's no good reason for this. One might cite the low numbers of women in the sciences and the military, but three credited roles compared to 32? Please.

Doctor Who is hardly unique in the appalling absence of women onscreen, of course; indeed television as a whole still falls far short from showing women as 50% of the characters we see. A recent study from Geena Davis's Institute on Gender in Media has found that today for every one speaking female character, there are roughly three speaking male ones[46]. And when we see group scenes, they are approximately 17% female[47]. (if you reach a level of 33% women, most people perceive women to be in the majority.) The research also found that these ratios have been the same since 1946.

---

[46] 'Gender Bias without Borders'. Geena Davis Institute on Gender in Media.

[47] Davis, Geena, 'Geena Davis' Two Easy Steps to Make Hollywood Less Sexist (Guest Column)'. *Hollywood Reporter*, 11 December 2013.

Let that sink in for a moment:

1946.

That's 70 years, for pity's sake.

Okay, so not a happy thought. It gets worse: if media don't bother to portray women being seen in equal numbers with men, it normalises fewer women being seen, so that when there is equality, both men and women tend to see that as being female-dominated.

This, as you might imagine, is a problem. A big one, one that spills out all over our society in ways that go way beyond the purview of this book. So let me bring this back round to *Ambassadors*. After seeing this report, Geena Davis called for two things that could simply and easily pushback against this entrenched bias against women and our representation in media. One, she suggested that anyone writing a play, film, book or whatever went through their work and added in female first names to half their characters. Secondly, she suggested that whenever there is a crowd scene, the directions explicitly state that it should be 50% women. Two very small things, neither adding dollar signs to production, but both ways to quickly and easily attack the problem. Now, a lovely thing about **Doctor Who** is that while there are ups and downs, one thing that has definitely improved over the past 50 years is the ratio of male to female characters. And while *Ambassadors* is woeful on the speaking parts for women, it was made 45 years ago so I feel I can cut it a little slack, and I do want to give it a nod of credit when it comes to the background artists. Throughout the story we get three different women in the background at Space Centre. It's a small thing, but it matters. It's still not an even split, there are definitely more men monitoring the space-y goings on, but it's about a third of the scientist extras we see, which is rather better than the average, and worth noting.

There are plenty of scenes in Space Centre where there's more than one woman present, and we do get one where there's equal split of men and women onscreen. We see the Doctor, Liz, and Cornish examining the capsule. There's also an extra, presumably another scientist working at Space Centre, and she's a woman. It's a single scene in a very lengthy story, but having the show leap that very low obstacle of equal representation, for even a moment, is a pleasure to see.

Of the two named speaking roles, both are scientists: Liz Shaw, a marvellously conceived character, and Miss Rutherford, who appears to be Cornish's number two. Women are, however, entirely absent from the military, the ministry, and the astronaut corps.

As well as Liz Shaw, a brilliant scientist in a variety of disciplines, season seven had the lovely habit of giving us a second female scientist in its stories. Here we have Miss Rutherford, who sadly disappears after episode two. She's the one who gives the Brigadier the answers to his questions about how and why they might have lost contact with Recovery 7. Like Cornish, despite the tense situation, she remains calm and matter-of-fact without. Exactly the sort of person you want on either end of a delicate space mission.

Liz Shaw is referred to as 'the girl', despite being an adult[48]. It's a common problem in a lot of 20th-century **Doctor Who**: the writers

---

[48] Once in each of episodes 3, 4 and 5.

seem to be allergic to the word 'woman'. Liz is always 'Miss Shaw', never 'Doctor Shaw,' despite the fact that its established in her first story she has a doctorate. This is often more grating than in *Ambassadors* – here Ralph Cornish the head of the Space Centre is often addressed as 'Mr Cornish', though episode 1 establishes that he's entitled to the title 'Professor'. There's also the British custom of having one's title revert to 'Ms' or 'Mr' if one becomes a surgeon, which could be used to excuse no-one ever addressing Liz Shaw – who holds a medical degree – by her title.

A good note, however, is Liz's loud verbal and physical rejection whenever she is touched and doesn't want to be. She is facing violent and dangerous men, and yet she still feels wholly entitled to exert control over her own body. Companions in **Doctor Who** are often grabbed by villains, but none so consistently enforce their own personal boundaries as Liz does in *Ambassadors*.

UNIT

There was something profoundly satisfying about watching one of the most recent UNIT stories, *The Zygon Invasion / The Zygon Inversion* (2015), and seeing every speaking role in UNIT, bar one, played by a woman. It felt validating in a way that television often doesn't, if you're a woman. And it made up a little bit for the dozens of **Doctor Who** stories where only one or two women were present.

The UNIT of season seven is an entirely male affair. It's led by Brigadier Lethbridge-Stewart, but the rest of the military characters, bar one, only stick around for a single story. Although, when most of the stories are seven episodes long, that does give them a little time to shine. *Ambassadors* also marks the return of Corporal Benton, now a sergeant. John Levene first appeared as Benton in the inaugural UNIT story, *The Invasion* (1968), and he'll be sticking around for the next seven seasons of the show until his rather lacklustre swansong in *The Android Invasion* (1975). He doesn't have much to do in *Ambassadors*, but what we do see is rather promising. The Brigadier is shown to trust his judgement: when Lennox turns up, it's Benton he makes contact with first, and the Brigadier wants to know Benton's assessment of the scientist before he speaks with him himself. Benton is also shown to be a decent, compassionate man. He speaks kindly to Lennox, answering his questions, and treating him gently – the man's clearly terrified, and Benton is sensitive to that fact, offering to get him a cup of tea and something to read.

UNIT as an organisation, however, has a few bumpy moments: numerous times, Reegan and his thugs are able to get inside and commit sabotage and murder. Even though Carrington, who would presumably be kept up to date with all the latest security measures, is feeding them information, it's still embarrassing that their fake passes and disguises keep working, even when UNIT is well aware of the danger.

Despite this, we're left with the impression that UNIT is an effective organisation. And, as with the rest of season seven, it very much feels here that the Doctor is acting as their scientific advisor, as opposed to UNIT providing the manpower to back up the Doctor's agenda. We also get a good sense of how UNIT might have coped without the Doctor's influence, and what the results would more often have been, with the Brigadier immediately applying a military solution when he discovers where the reply to the alien message is coming from: UNIT troops plough into the warehouse, guns ready, and are immediately fired upon. Naturally, they fire back, people are killed. There's a rather nasty shot that implies a man's lost his fingers without actually showing it, or any blood. When the two forces close in on each other, a number of brutal fist fights occur. The most telling moment comes when the Brigadier stands face to face with one of the civilians, each of them pointing a gun at the other. 'You kill me, my men kill you – pointless really,' he says[49]. The thoughtful soldier acknowledges the vicious circle of violence begetting more violence.

---

[49] Episode one.

BRITISH SPACE PROGRAMMES, REAL AND FICTIONAL

Ambassadors opens focussed on an astronaut on board a space capsule – a British astronaut. The first British astronaut wouldn't enter space until 1991, when Helen Sharman went up on the Russian Soyuz TM-12 mission. And this astronaut is communicating with a British Ground Control. This is the near future, and one that never came to pass: we're seeing a manned mission to Mars in the 1970s or 80s, depending on who's writing the timeline.

Today this seems far-fetched. After all, no-one's been to the Moon in over 40 years, and since when did the UK have its own space project? If anything, seeing a purely British presence in space tends to be a clue that we're involved in an alternate universe sci-fi scenario, perhaps one where the British Empire maintained its stranglehold on a third of the planet, and has now expanded its grasp into space.

In 1970, however, things were a little different. We were smack bang in the middle of that magical time window when humanity wasn't just sending people into orbit; we were sending people to the Moon too. In fact, while *Ambassadors* was being broadcast in the UK, suggesting we'd made it to Mars, on the other side of the planet NASA had just launched the Apollo 13 mission to send another three astronauts to land on the moon. Famously, they never made it, thanks to an oxygen tank failure (which occurred between episodes 4 and 5 of *Ambassadors*), and they almost never made it back to Earth either. But astronauts have always known the risks of going into space. And this near miss didn't stop NASA greenlighting another four missions to the Moon.

As for Britain, well, there was indeed a purely British space programme, though its goals were a little less ambitious.

By 1958, the British rocket programme was up and running, and we had developed our own homemade rockets: the Black Knights[50]. These were designed, built, and tested in the UK, then transported to Australia for launch. The test flights were successful: two launched without payload, to prove the rocket could actually fly, then a re-entry vehicle was attached, and shown to be successful. Testing continued on different designs for the nosecone of the rocket, but before any further development could be done into using the Black Knight to launch a satellite, funding was cut by the Government, in favour of the Black Arrow project, which began in 1964[51].

During the time of the Black Knights, the United Kingdom did, briefly get a satellite in orbit. After the United States and the Soviet Union, we became the third country to operate our own satellite. It was British-made, but launched by NASA from Cape Canaveral. It was called Ariel 1, and sadly, lasted less than three months before it was accidently nuked by the Americans.

The Black Arrow rockets, like the Knights, were all launched at Woomera, in Australia[52], though a launch site in Norfolk was considered, but the risk to North Sea oil drilling was considered too great.

---

[50] Hill, CN, *A Vertical Empire: The History of the UK Rocket and Space Programme, 1950-1971*, p6.
[51] Hill, *A Vertical Empire*, p7.
[52] Hill, *A Vertical Empire*, p13.

Orba was meant to be the first British satellite put in orbit by a British rocket (it also had the rather cooler name X-2) , but when it blasted off in 1970, the second stage of the Black Arrow rocket shut down early, and it lacked the velocity to reach orbit[53]. It was clear by this time that Britain's space program was going nowhere: there was never any funding, or intention, for there to be any sort of British astronaut program (the UK didn't even provide any money for the International Space Station until 2011) and the Orba was facing major restrictions in funding, with the Treasury in staunch opposition to spending any more money on it[54]. The Black Arrow project was cancelled, with virtually no interest from the public or press, in July 1971[55], little more than a year after *Ambassadors* was broadcast, but one last launch was scheduled, to occur after the official cancellation.

This final launch was the Prospero 1 – named after the character in Shakespeare's *The Tempest*. The name was changed to that of the sorcerer preparing to give up his powers after the Black Arrow programme was cancelled; previously, the satellite had been named Puck, from *A Midsummer Night's Dream*, while the first satellite, Ariel, had been named for the spirit bound to serve Prospero.

Prospero 1 was a British-made and operated satellite being put into orbit on a British-made rocket. It was to be the final, and most successful, launch of the wholly British space programme[56]. It even managed to avoid getting damaged by the Americans. (It did

---

[53] Hill, *A Vertical Empire*, p309.
[54] Hill, *A Vertical Empire*, p312.
[55] Hill, *A Vertical Empire*, p318.
[56] Hill, *A Vertical Empire*, p310.

however, sustain a serious whack from its own launch rocket, as the third stage of the Black Arrow, the Waxwing, entered orbit rather faster than expected.) As of 2015, we have the dubious honour of being the only country in the world to develop and operate an independent satellite launch programme, and then abandon it.

Prospero is still up there. It was officially deactivated in 1996, but in some years it gets turned back on for its anniversary. Its orbit isn't expected to decay until 2070, almost 100 years after it was first launched.

Concurrently with the independent British space capability, there was interest in joint European projects. We see a nod to this in *Ambassadors*, with the French scientist Taltalian heavily involved in the Space Centre, which may very well be an Anglo-French project rather than a purely British one.

The first joint European space project developed out of a failed British project to build ballistic missiles: the designs couldn't compete with the stuff the Americans and Soviets were making, and so the project was abandoned. In an attempt to salvage something from it, a proposal was put to the French, and a design was agreed in 1964[57]. This first European project was eventually named Europa, and its development came under the auspices of the European Launcher Development Organisation (ELDO), consisting of six European nations, with Australia as an associate

---

[57] Hill, *A Vertical Empire*, p213.

who contributed an initial launching and test site[58]. Launches would later move to French Guiana.

The Europa 1 project cost the European nations millions, but after 10 years still failed to provide a reliable means to get satellites into orbit. Attempts at Europa 2 were abandoned, along with ELDO.[59]

The successor to the Europa project was the Ariane rocket, developed by the newly formed European Space Agency (ESA), and owned primarily by France. The first successful launch occurred on 24 December 1974[60]. Since then, the Ariane rocket has been redesigned several times, and today ESA launches its payloads on the Ariane 5. Hundreds of satellites and hundreds of thousands of kilograms of equipment have been delivered into orbit by the Ariane launch system[61], and it's been over a decade since there was a failed Ariane launch.[62]

European astronauts have gone into space on flights in co-operation with NASA and the Soviet Union (now Russia), some of these missions fully funded by the ESA. They became common enough that Europe founded its own astronaut centre in 1990. There are currently 15 ESA astronauts, including Samantha Cristoforetti, who holds the record for the longest uninterrupted spaceflight of any European.

---

[58] Hill, *A Vertical Empire*, p212.
[59] Hill, *A Vertical Empire*, p224.
[60] 'A Look at the Past'. ESA.
[61] 'Ariane 4'. ESA.
[62] 'Ariane 5'. ESA.

France did try for an independent European crewed spaceflight capability[63], but while this project, Hermes, was in development, the Cold War was declared at an end, and the possibility of much closer co-operation with Russia was opened up. The Hermes project was abandoned.

In the past few years, ESA has joined NASA's Orion programme[64], intended to be the next phase of crewed spaceflight, though it won't be going to Mars. The willingness to meet the costs, and the technology, still aren't within our reach.

In the aftermath of World War II, the United Kingdom was no longer a superpower, but it took a while for the fiction to catch up with reality. (And the country itself remained in denial in many ways[65].) This gave us a marvellous decade or two where it was entirely acceptable, even believable for the reader, for science fiction stories to posit a future where the UK was a space power, with its own independent launch capability and astronaut corps. The two most significant narratives, ones which are still enjoyed today, were the adventures of Dan Dare, a daring British space pilot, and Professor Bernard Quatermass, who heads the British space programme.

Both **Dan Dare** and **Quatermass** first appeared in the 1950s, and are clear inspiration for the slightly futuristic UK we see in season seven, and in *Ambassadors* in particular. Quatermass, in particular,

---

[63] 'History: Hermes Spaceplane, 1987'. ESA.

[64] 'Orion'. ESA.

[65] For instance, one reason we developed an independent nuclear weapon was to get in the Nuclear Club, with the USA and the Soviet Union (*A Vertical Empire*, p3).

could easily wander into Space Centre and be quite at home. And his stories have a heavy influence on much of **Doctor Who**: he too faced terrifying, unearthly threats to mankind that could only be stopped with his intelligence and the power of science. Season seven, with its serious tone, lengthy stories, and Earth setting, at times feels almost a homage to those 50s serials.

Quatermass also sticks closely to reality in its setup. Indeed, one could easily see this as the path taken if the British Government had decided to make funding for the space programme its priority. In the first serial, **The Quatermass Experiment** (1953), the British Rocket Group launches from Australia, as the actual British space programme did. Its crewed missions are modest: a three-person crew to go into orbit around the Earth, then return. **Quatermass II** (1955) pushes things a little further – there are plans for Moon bases. And **Quatermass and the Pit** (1958-59), the third and final of the original television serials, sees another nod to reality as Quatermass is furious at his funding being cut.

Dan Dare, too, cared about plausibility. The first strip had Arthur C Clarke acting as scientific advisor. Looking back from the modern day, it feels more outlandish than **Quatermass**: our hero travelled between the planets of our solar system, and all were assumed to have life (a common enough assumption in science fiction prior to the first space probes reaching these worlds). In the very first strip, this intrepid 'Biggles in space' successfully pilots the first crewed mission to Venus. Interestingly, despite his status as an officer in the Interplanet Space Fleet, a military organisation whose uniforms riffed off those of the British army, Dan Dare leaned towards non-violent resolutions for the problems he encountered.

The progress of the British space programme as presented in *The Ambassadors of Death* falls somewhere in between Quatermass's crewed Earth orbits, and Dare's interplanetary adventures. In episode one, we're heading for Mars, and it's quickly made clear this isn't even the first crewed mission there. While the previous missions are implied to be successful, in Mars Probe 7, **something** has gone wrong. They've arrived back in Earth orbit, but communications remain silent. We have a nod to our space allies – 'Can't the Americans do anything?' asks Cornish, but sadly NASA doesn't have a rescue vehicle ready to launch either[66] – we seem to be the only ones out there. It's a glorious opening to the story, managing to be tense and intriguing drama while exposition is dropping seamlessly into the drama to catch us up on what's happening. And it does two things that remind me why **Doctor Who** is my very favourite of all television shows.

First, this is all done on the cheap: no special effects, no lovely shots of a planet or rocket ships. Nope, we've got two close-up shots of two men talking to each other. One of them is in a spacesuit, and we hear his voice through a radio just as mission control would. And yet, it feels **real**. The tension is palpable. It's a credit to the actors and the director, Michael Ferguson, how much they can do with so little. Secondly, these images evoke a nostalgia in me for a lost past, an impossible past. I'm not inclined much towards that sort of thing: there is much awfulness in the present, but it still looks a lot shinier to me than any other decade. I like my antibiotics and clean running water and dental healthcare and right to equal pay. But here I find an exception. A British space

---

[66] Episode one.

programme! A British space programme so wildly successful we're sending people to Mars! And we can rescue them too! Twice! How ridiculously wonderful.

While real life has not exactly followed what the fiction of the early decades of the Cold War predicted – first, the Moon, then Mars, then beyond! And possibly aliens too – what has happened and what we have discovered have still been extraordinary. Television never predicted how our basic understanding of the universe would expand and deepen thanks to projects like the Hubble telescope and the Space Lab which were among the many joint ESA-NASA projects, or the International Space Station, partly funded by the ESA. We have, through our involvement in space, pushed human achievement and knowledge forward. We may not have visited any extrasolar planets, but we know that they're out there now. And silly as what much of what we once dreamed of looks now, these were the stories that today's scientists and astronauts and engineers grew up on, and the stories we tell today will be the ones that inspire the next generation of explorers.

As the story comes to a close, journalist John Wakefield attempts to make a worldwide telecast, a satellite-facilitated transmission that is only possible because of the space programmes that took weapons of mass destruction – missiles – and transformed them into rockets that could reach outer space.

Season seven has a unique structure in the manner in which the episodes are broken up into longer stories. Gone are the days of **Doctor Who** being on television for 48 weeks of the year. Instead, that's been almost halved down to 25 episodes. This gives the stories room to breathe, to build tension – and, yes, plenty of space for padding as the writers realise they've run out of plot. But while that was a serious problem in later Pertwee six-parters, the seven-parters of season seven never feel sluggish to me: languid, perhaps, and they might meander a little, but it always feels like it's done in a deliberate, considered way. Nothing to compare to the Doctor's four-hour swordfight in *The Monster of Peladon* (1974), or the episode of *Planet of the Spiders* (1974) that's one endless, tedious chase scene[67]. The pacing works particularly well in *Ambassadors*, since it feels just right for the space missions.

It begins right from the start in the slow, but oh-so good, opening episode. Space missions **are** slow, and while some adjustments have to be made for the sake of drama, having this section of the story edge forward inch by inch makes for wonderful viewing, especially if you're a habitual watcher of the actual space mission videos NASA puts out. The tension ramps up so incrementally as the Recovery 7 rocket reaches Mars Probe 7, as the Doctor gets drawn into watching the mission, as we link up, and the reason for this mission is revealed... I'm only sad I never got to watch this story unspoiled. It's a mystery, but extra exciting for being set in space, for having the only people who can help hundreds of miles and a rocket launch away.

Episode 1, however, does finish with an almost modern feel to the pacing. While many questions are left unanswered, UNIT manage to track down the exact location of the reply to the mysterious message. It is, not too surprisingly, in an abandoned warehouse,

---

[67] *The Monster of Peladon* Episode four; *Planet of the Spiders* Episode two. (NB Durations may be exaggerated for rhetorical effect. But only a bit.)

almost within walking distance of the Space Centre. Here we see two men, one wearing a fetching bright red carnation, at a radio set, sending a second reply. Moments later, no fewer than three jeeps packed with UNIT soldiers, and led by Lethbridge-Stewart, arrive at the warehouse and one of the more impressive firefights in 20th-century **Doctor Who** takes place.

In episode 2, Recovery 7 comes back down to Earth. As with Mars Probe 7, all contact has been lost. Are the astronauts still alive? Or is there something else in the capsule? Will they even make it down to Earth alive? It's a wonderfully tense sequence, that consists of a lot of close-ups of different characters, and a subtly shifting mood in the control room as the capsule is brought down. It's some truly fantastic work from all the actors involved, as they all remain calm professionals doing their job, while still showing the atmosphere shifts from one of tense expectation and dread to hope, relief and a bit of cheer as the capsule finally makes it back to Earth.

CLASS DIVISIONS

'I've known Bruno Taltalian for years,' is probably the most telling line in the story in terms of what it has to say about class. Bruno Taltalian turns out to be a man who will lie, steal, threaten, and murder, but does it matter? Not to Sir James Quinlan, because he **knows** the man, you see. The 'top man' is incredulous regarding Taltalian's criminal behaviour because Taltalian is (in the commonly used phrase) 'one of us', in the old boy's network, known to the establishment, and so despite the harm he's done the establishment is unwilling to move against him.

The one action Quinlan will take is to 'initiate a top-level investigation'. Investigations, reports, committees; they're all markers for bureaucratic inertia, and criticism of the British political class and civil service. The Doctor's recognises this response for what it is, and enquires acidly, 'is that all you've got to say, Sir James? Sweep it all under the carpet, eh?'[68] The Brigadier too, recognises the issues but he is much more a part of the establishment, and sees aggravating Sir James as a futile gesture.

When confronted with unequivocal proof of the infiltration at the Space Centre, and the other shady goings-on and his part in them, Sir James is utterly unrepentant. He doesn't blink at being accused, or having explanations demanded of him. He is at ease with the power he has, and the way in which he's abused it. He doesn't believe he's done anything wrong, nor is there a hint that that he's worried about any repercussions.

---

[68] Episode two.

Sir James is part of the upper middle class: a high-ranking civil servant, and a knight of the realm. He's also very firmly entrenched in, and committed to, the established power-structure of British society. On the other side, our heroes are all outsiders in some way. Liz Shaw is a woman, and a woman in the hard sciences no less. And this is set around 1970 too, the Equal Pay Act has only just been passed[69], and women make up less than a third of university students obtaining their first degree, and a mere tenth of those obtaining a higher degree[70]. The Doctor is an alien, unwillingly exiled to Earth, and dependent upon the Brigadier's protection and goodwill for scientific equipment and a laboratory to work on repairing the TARDIS. Even the Brigadier, the most establishment of the three figures, is fingered as an outsider by his superior, General Carrington: Lethbridge-Stewart is an officer in an international organisation, not a British one, and so he gets tarnished with the implication that he's not really 'one of us'.

There's also a significant contrast in attitudes towards the general public between Sir James and Carrington on the one hand, and Cornish and the Space Centre on the other. Cornish has arranged a live broadcast from mission control during an important mission, keeping everyone bang up to date even when stuff goes wrong. Sir James, on the other hand, is committed to keeping information away from people. 'We don't want the public to become panic-stricken,' he says, perfectly calmly. The public are, of course, not as bright as Sir James, who knows what's best, I'm sure, and has a

---

[69] And yet still, 45 years later, not properly enforced.
[70] Bolton, Paul, 'Education: Historical Statistics – November 2012'. Digital Education Resource Archive.

radiation-proof bunker and plenty of private doctors he can afford, should he need them. I imagine.

This is seen again when Cornish, magnificently, tells Sir James in 1970 daytime telly speak, to sod off, he's launching a rescue rocket. His weapon? The press. Unless Sir James gives permission, Cornish will call a press conference and let everyone know exactly what's going on. Once again, we see the divide between politics and science, between openness and freedom of information, and closed doors and backroom dealing.

We're also witness to some of the more subtle forms of power: when attempting to launch a second rescue, Cornish finds that 'everything is taking just that bit longer than it should.'[71] He suspects Sir James, but he cannot prove it. It's not hard to imagine Sir James sitting behind his desk, making a few phone calls, calling a few people 'old chap', and asking for a couple of favours. Just enough to slow down the efforts of the rescue launch, nothing terrible you understand, just giving us a bit of time... the combined efforts of numerous people slowing down just a bit could be devastating, of course. We see here, in a few short words the insidious power of the social network a man like Sir James has access to in action.

Eventually, the killer blow comes when Sir James manages to arrange that every astronaut available to Ralph Cornish isn't able to take part in the mission: they're not in good enough health, or they've been transferred, or they're waiting for a security clearance. All problems easy enough to arrange if you're a puppeteer with plenty of strings to pull on.

---

[71] Episode three.

When the UNIT team are fed a stack of lies by Sir James, it's the Doctor, arguably the most privileged of the three even without his TARDIS, who insists on proof. The Doctor, as a character, is enormously privileged: he's not just male, white, and able-bodied, he – mostly – has no dependence on material wealth, and the freedom to roam the universe. At his worst, he's reminiscent of some upper-class explorer of the British Empire, off to teach the natives how to lead good, Christian lives; at his best he inserts himself in between those who have power and those who the ones with power are trying to hurt. He remains a privileged individual, but he uses that privilege as a shield or barrier to protect those who cannot protect themselves from those who would abuse their power.

Sir James's last resort is that 'we could tell him the truth.' The truth, the last line of defence, when, as Sir James puts it, there's 'no alternative'[72]. He seems to go with this option and invites the Doctor to come and hear the truth, just before he's murdered by an Ambassador. Sir James could hardly be called a villain, not in the traditional sense, but he is part of a more banal evil: those with power who assume they should have it, that they may use it as they choose without consequence, and that they know best. He is part of an entrenched political class that is poison to any free and open society, with a paternalistic view of those whom he is meant to serve. He is the might of the bureaucratic inertia of the civil service.[73]

---

[72] Episode four.

[73] For probably the very best look at this sort of thing, might I recommend **Yes Minister** (1980-84), and its superb sequel, **Yes, Prime Minister** (1986-88).

But even the Doctor's not averse to taking advantage of bureaucracy and the inertia it creates when he suggests to Carrington that if he wants the rocket launch stopped, he takes the matter up with Quinlan's 'successor... when he's been appointed.'[74]

The scientific world, on the other hand, gets a good showing throughout the story. There are a plethora of scientists, and almost every one from the Doctor and Liz Shaw down manages to be a hero in their own way. Even the disgraced scientist Lennox, before his escape to UNIT, insists on examining the mysterious astronauts in his care, convinced by the radiation readings that something's wrong and they need help. Taltalian betrays his scientific team by attempting to destroy information, but he still shows an element of tribalism when he tells the Doctor 'I would not have used that gun, not on a fellow scientist.' Otherwise, the scientists – the Doctor, Liz Shaw, Ralph Cornish, Miss Rutherford, the ill-fated Professor Heldorf – are shown being honest and open with their knowledge and expertise. The most effective progress in science requires collaboration, the sharing of knowledge, and building on the work of those who came before. The conditions for scientific progress to flourish are in opposition to those that a self-selecting elite requires to stay in power.

It's important to note that while there are class divides evident in *Ambassadors*, they are relatively fine distinctions. We can condemn those motivated by money because to the best of our knowledge, they are seeking vast wealth, they want to rob Fort Knox and have more gold than they know what to do with. 'You were a respected scientist once,' Liz tells Lennox, appalled that he's sold himself out.

---

[74] Episode five.

'Grossly underpaid,' he shoots back[75]. Money as motivation is a trait shared by the antagonistic characters in this story, but we shouldn't forget that judging what others are willing to do for money can often be the purview of those who've never felt the lack of it. Principles are all very well, but they don't pay the rent or put food on the table. Everyone in *Ambassadors* – military, scientific, political and criminal – has a middle-class English accent; they are seeing everything from a relatively wealthy, comfortable middle-class point-of-view, and invite the audience to do so as well.

---

[75] Episode four.

THE AMBASSADORS

For most of the story, the Ambassadors exist as a blank slate for other characters to project their fears, or ambitions, on to. They're also the heart of the mystery that plays out, and it isn't until the Doctor finally meets them that all the questions are finally answered.

When we first see the Ambassadors, we have no reason not to believe they're the three astronauts who are still somehow alive despite having received lethal doses of radiation. Indeed Professor Heldorf, who is treating them, believes them to be human and insists on the proper treatment for victims of massive radiation poisoning. Carrington instructs him otherwise, insisting that Heldorf doesn't understand what has happened, that this is a new kind of radiation that the astronauts are now dependent upon and must be fed in order to live. That perversity of logic plays in rather well with the story's themes: the attack of the acceptance of logic twisted by fear – in order to save those people, you must try to kill them. In order to maintain peace, we must be ready for war. In order to be safe and free, we must make laws that violate and oppress.

Initially, the Ambassadors say nothing, and do very little. They lie down, they walk, they emit radiation, and they get sick when they don't have access to high levels of it. In the spacesuits, faceless and expressionless and silent, they're an intimidating presence. But that's small potatoes beside the fact that their very existence is toxic to any human that stays in close proximity to them, and we can't even see what it is that would kill us. They're immune to bullets (naturally), and can kill with a single touch. Rather than just have the monsters immune to bullets without rhyme or reason, in the earliest days of modern-day Earth invasion stories the point gets a bit of attention. The Brigadier finds flattened bullets that have been fired at the Ambassadors, and the Doctor surmises that they've been deflected by 'some sort of force field'[76], a somewhat more satisfying explanation for the Ambassador's invulnerability than they just happen to have bulletproof skin that also bulletproofs the human spacesuits they're wearing. (And a nice bit of Holmes and Watson style investigation from the Doctor and the Brig.)

When communication with the Ambassadors succeeds, the first thing they say is 'Why are we kept prisoners? Why do you make us kill? We are Ambassadors and came in peace.'[77] They don't want to kill, but they're not prepared to refrain from killing if it means their own deaths. While this is hardly an alien attitude, it's a nicely nuanced one, particularly for **Doctor Who** – they're peaceful, but they're not martyrs; they're come in peace, but they act first in the interests of their own survival.

We also have here a rare instance (and possibly one brought about by the Time Lords' interference with, and disabling parts of, the TARDIS), where the Doctor can't rely on his usual ability to understand and be understood by other species. It gives the Ambassadors a distance and feel of real otherworldliness often denied the aliens in **Doctor Who**, which is particularly ironic given that the Ambassadors are only seen in the spacesuits of human astronauts.

---

[76] Episode five.
[77] Episode seven.

81

And there is something wonderfully spooky about the unseen person in the spacesuit, especially walking around in a modern-day setting. As the Ambassadors are forced to attack, it's easy to see why Steven Moffat would bring back this image for the Vashta Nerada in *Silence in the Library / Forest of the Dead* (2008), and for the Doctor's mysterious killer in *The Impossible Astronaut / Day of the Moon* (2011).

The Ambassadors are only seen properly once, when for a few seconds in episode 6, one of the astronauts removes his helmet. Beneath, we find a human-ish head, with a discernible nose, mouth and two eyes, but the skin is bulbous and pocked, like the surface of the Moon, and both hair and skin are blue. It's superb make-up though, and worthy of far more than the few brief seconds we get to see it for. Perhaps it was considered too frightening for young children. It's enough to give Liz a bit of a fright, anyway.

For most of the story, the Ambassadors are also treated as tools, not people. They're activated by a touch of a button, and controlled by a remote. It's only when a more sophisticated communications device is built, and language humans can understand, as well as two-way communication, becomes possible that they shift into becoming people. This is reflected in the language used to refer to them too. Their captors call them 'creatures', and once they're used on raids, this othering language is used by the UNIT teams as well[78]. Carrington calls them 'monsters'. In the final moments, however, their personhood is properly acknowledged at last, as the Doctor, referring to the last captured Ambassador, asks someone to 'please release that

---

[78] Episodes 4 and 5.

gentleman.' Cornish too, hesitates before naming them, finally settling on 'Ambassadors'[79]. They are no longer creatures, or monsters; they are people.

There's really only one false note in the treatment of the aliens in this story, and it comes when the Alien Space Captain claims they have the power to destroy Earth, and threatens to do so if the Ambassadors are not returned. In an otherwise nuanced and realistic story, this seems rather heavy-handed. I know as we approach the climax of the story upping the stakes is the sort of thing generally needed for drama, but given that, we can be pretty certain the Earth isn't going to be destroyed[80] and it's hardly a proportional response to the capture of three Ambassadors. Indeed this threat lends a sliver of credibility to Carrington's position. What if the Ambassadors had been killed at some point, what then? Do you tell the aliens and risk them attacking, or attack them first, and hope the advantage of first strike will be enough to overcome their superior technology?

---

[79] Episode seven.

[80] I say 'pretty certain' – after all, there was that one time when the whole universe got blown up, including Earth, in *The Big Bang* (2010).

THE ABSENT TARDIS

In contrast to the mysterious aliens, what would have been the most familiar element of the show to the original viewers, the TARDIS, is largely absent from *Ambassadors*. Formerly such a fundamental part of the show, our touchstone of normality, of home, is seen only perfunctorily to remind us why the Doctor's always on modern day Earth these days.

This is also the first time we see the TARDIS console in colour, and it's the console that was used in the black-and-white era. In colour, the seemingly white console is now slightly green, since white had a tendency to flare on black-and-white television. And the console is sitting in a contemporary room, not the console room of the TARDIS. While this might have been done to save money – the console room set of the black-and-white era surely wouldn't have stood up to colour scrutiny – it also serves to remove an element of the fantastic – the bigger-on-the-inside-than-the-outside TARDIS – from a story very heavy on the realism.

What we do get, however, is for something a little bit 'Who-ish' to happen, as Terrance Dicks puts it on the commentary, right at the beginning of the story, just to remind the viewer that they're watching the right channel. In trying to 'reactivate the TARDIS's time vector generator' there are a few moments of time-travel, as the Doctor sends himself and Liz Shaw a few seconds into the future[81]. But this is played for amusement: a silly diversion before we get down to the serious business of the real story. Liz herself mocks the Doctor for thinking he can mess around with time like he

---

[81] Episode one.

suggests, and even when it happens, she clearly leans towards the side of thinking he's lost it rather than believe his explanation.

COLOUR SEPARATION OVERLAY, AND OTHER SPECIAL EFFECTS

This was a time when CSO, standing for Colour Separation Overlay, was all the rage in **Doctor Who**. It was a brand-new technique and the production team were not afraid to experiment. While we don't reach the giddy heights of season eight's use (a kitchen! An evil troll doll! A tiny dead corpse in a lunchbox![82]) it's still in evidence here. Used rather well, I think, in an establishing shot of mission control to give the place a little more height and a pentagonal dome roof that feels rather retro-futuristic.

There's also some wonderful model work as the Recovery 7 capsule links up with Mars Probe 7. It looks dated, sure – it's been 45 years after all. But model work, even relatively cheap model work, ages remarkably well, especially compared to computer-generated imagery. Also, a shout-out to the incidental music here. After the, ah, experimental noise of the previous story, it's a delight to hear Dudley Simpson being rather more restrained and subtle for the space shots here, in a music choice clearly influenced by 1968's *2001: A Space Odyssey*, where the 'Blue Danube' waltz is played as two spaceships complete the precise and delicate manoeuvres needed to facilitate a linkup.

No money to show the lack of gravity? No worries, just have your astronaut crawl to the space lock, then we'll flip the shot upside down! He'll look like he's floating on the ceiling![83]

---

[82] All in *Terror of the Autons*.

[83] You have no idea how betrayed I felt as I child when I found out this was how Batman and Robin – Adam West and Burt Ward, the

For triangulating the origin of the reply message, we don't merely get a rather handy map on the wall showing where the radio telescopes are, we get shots of various radio telescopes from around the world: one is shrouded with snow and ice, another has the New Zealand flag flying nearby. But the signal is, of course, coming from the Home Counties. London, to be exact. This is, after all, Pertwee-era **Who**. The Recovery 7 capsule, too, lands 'somewhere in the south of England'[84]. And, again, within easy driving distance of Space Centre.

The Recovery 7 capsule itself is rather lovely. It's big and silver and looks superb set against some of the wilder countryside of southern England. It looks solid too, surrounded by UNIT jeeps, and its weight is given due consideration, as the story has the budget for a lorry with a crane attached to lift the capsule onto its back.

The lift-off of the second rescue mission, with the Doctor on board, is rather less successful, effects-wise. The brief look we get of the rocket during the first phase is sorely unconvincing. Rather better are the shots inside the capsule where we see the Doctor's pained expression as the G-force hits and he experiences gravity multiple times that of Earth. For once, Pertwee's habit of gurning is put to excellent use.

The alien spaceship has an interesting design, one that seems to inspire the much more fully realised Axos, a living ship, in the following season's The Claws of Axos (1971). The use of light, shape, and colour suggest the organic, in contrast to the shining

---

best ones, obviously – managed so much effortless climbing up skyscrapers in **Batman** (1966-68).

[84] Episode two.

silver and blunt angles of the British rockets. There's also a hint of the original **Star Trek**'s *The Doomsday Machine* (1967) about it that adds an aura of menace to its approach if you're familiar with that episode.

GENRE

Doctor Who is of course a science-fiction show, and season seven is even more science-fiction than most **Doctor Who**. But being stuck in a near-contemporary 1970ish Earth, it's easy to mix in a few other genres. In *Ambassadors*, we have elements of the snazzy gadgetry and undercover derring-do of slick 1960s spy series like **The Avengers** (1961-69) and **The Man from UNCLE** (1964-68), merged with the grit and grime of 70s detective shows such as **The Sweeney** or **The Professionals** (1977-1983).

Though the villains' underground base is hardly up to Bond-villain standard, they do have plenty of impressive equipment. The first location we see is a grim abandoned warehouse, but even there, they've got a self-destruct mechanism attached to their equipment and a secret exit, in case of emergencies. More impressively, they have access to a helicopter that swoops in while UNIT are retrieving Recovery 7. And the people on board come with enough firepower to force the UNIT convoy off the road, defeat the escort's soldiers, and steal the space capsule. They drop smoke bombs, and they're fighting with guns that fire some sort of invisible energy and can be used to stun opponents.

There are no expensive cars to dash around in, but Bessie does have some upgrades worthy of Q. The anti-theft device is a switch that leaves any would-be-thieves stuck to the car. And the baddies get themselves a van that can somehow get a new paint job in a matter of seconds.

There are double-agents aplenty, or at least people being paid to spy when they should be concentrating on the science. Liz's borrowed lab assistant, Dobson, reports in to Carrington's lot, while

Taltalian sabotages his own computer to try and stop her decoding work. The ante is upped when even the 'top man', Sir James, is seen towards the end of episode 2 to be in collusion with Carrington. The number of people in on the conspiracy to some extent helps to explain why so many bad guys are able to pass themselves off as UNIT soldiers. More mundanely, the villains also send a convincing message purporting to be from the Brigadier, one that's believed by the Doctor and Liz. They even have particularly nasty, inventive ways of killing people: poor old Lennox is murdered via radiation poisoning when someone plants a highly radioactive isotope in his cell, disguised as dinner.

Intertwined with grit and flash on the ground, we also have a gorgeous mystery that is teased out extremely well over the seven episodes. It's a wonderful matryoshka doll of a story, with the satisfaction of each reveal or success leading to another intriguing question.

The aspect of the mystery that still gives me shivers, even after multiple re-watches, is what happens in the aftermath of the Recovery 7 capsule coming down. UNIT heads out to retrieve it, along with Ralph Cornish, but the capsule remains closed, locked from the inside. And, at first, it doesn't even respond to attempts to communicate with the people we hope are within. Simply cutting the capsule open is initially dismissed as being too dangerous to the astronauts, but after hours of effort and no response, Cornish agrees to attempt to break in using thermal lances. But before he can send for them there is, at last, a response: 'Hello, Space Centre, this is Recovery 7, would you clear us for re-entry,' is the long-awaited reply[85]. There is triumph on the expression of our regulars, and even Cornish breaks into a smile, certain he's got at least one astronaut back alive. Unfortunately it quickly becomes clear the message they're receiving is a recording being repeated over and over again. The capsule is cut open, and inside, it's empty.

This reveal, naturally, raises more questions than it resolves, deepening the mystery, while still providing the satisfaction of an answer. It intrigues, and it's also just a little bit frightening. Those astronauts are still missing, and some intelligence has gone to a lot of trouble to delay our heroes. Who are they? What do they want? These fundamental questions lie untouched an hour into *Ambassadors*, and yet there's no feeling of being cheated out of answers, or off any of the characters being passed the idiot ball to slow things down.

One reveal that sadly lacks punch is who the leader of the mysterious plotters is. We see Carrington in charge of the attacks on UNIT several times, but the revelation that he is a British officer, a general indeed, occurs very casually as he simply appears onscreen in uniform at the lab where the three astronauts kidnapped from Recovery 7 have been taken.

The mystery appears to come to an end in episode 3, as our heroes confront Sir James, and he's unable to fob them off again: they have too much evidence that someone further up the ladder is involved, and so he presents General Carrington, who manages to explain away everything that's happened so far. It sounds quite good: it was for security, there's a mysterious new, contagious

---

[85] Episode two.

radiation that the astronauts have been infected with that could spread like a plague, we really were doing it all to help, you know. Of course, he's lying. And if the Doctor doesn't know for certain, he's quite rightly suspicious.

As the politics change on the ground, and the Ambassadors are sent out to kill, the space mystery slides into the backseat. The focus shifts to trying to find the Ambassadors and, when that leads to dead ends, to get another rocket ready for launch. After a gap of several episodes, we find ourselves back where we were in episode one – a rescue capsule has docked with Mars Probe 7 and the pilot is about to go on board and find out what's happened to the astronauts. In the time in between the situation has been somewhat illuminated, but we still have no information on what's happened to these guys, or even whether they're still alive.

The space adventure notches up when the Doctor's attempt to board Mars Probe 7 is interrupted by another object on a collision course. The audience gets a look at it, the Doctor's view of it from the rescue ship, and it's clearly something quite inhuman. The perspective then shifts to ground control, and we watch along with those in the Space Centre as the new spaceship appears to crash with Mars Probe 7.

Of course, that's not what happens; at last, the reason for the silence of Mars Probe 7 is revealed: the astronauts are the prisoners of aliens they met on Mars, and the aliens want to know why their Ambassadors have not been returned. Naturally enough, until they can secure the safety of their own people, they've kept hold of the humans.

A CRUMB OF DISCONTINUITY

In the seventh Doctor story *Remembrance of the Daleks* (1988), there's an in-joke, a reference to 'Bernard' and his 'British Rocket Group'. Bernard is Professor Bernard Quatermass, and the Rocket Group is the British space programme that he leads in the three **Quatermass** serials of the 1950s[86]. Those serials have clearly had a strong influence on all the stories of season seven (it wouldn't be much of a stretch to rewrite them with Quatermass instead of the Doctor), but in the expanded **Doctor Who** universe of the tie-in novels and audio dramas they've been given an even closer relationship: the British Rocket Group was renamed the British Space Centre and headed up by Ralph Cornish, before the name reverted back to the British Rocket Group again. While there are references in various audios and books[87], we don't hear about them on television again, but if you watch *The Christmas Invasion* (2005) closely, you can spot the British Rocket Group logo in the background, as they're the team responsible for launching the Guinevere One Satellite.

---

[86] **The Quatermass Experiment, Quatermass II** and **Quatermass and the Pit.**

[87] The BRG is referenced in the Big Finish audio series **Counter-Measures** (2012-), as well as the **Doctor Who** audio, *The Feast of Axos* (2011), the Virgin novels *Who Killed Kennedy?* (1996) and *The Dying Days* (1997), and the BBC novel *Loving the Alien* (2003).

CONCLUSION

Let me tell you a secret: I was worried that after writing tens of thousands of words about the story, I would hate *Ambassadors*. Focussing in on a single story in such detail, watching it again and again, examining it, analysing it, dissecting it. Surely, whatever was left at the end of this wouldn't be a pretty picture?

But it is. *Ambassadors* has been my favourite of season seven since I first watched it, and putting it under such close scrutiny has only increased my admiration and love for it. It's a complicated, nuanced story that explores humanity's conflicted, messy reactions to the unknown, and comes down firmly on the side of patience, knowledge, curiosity and trust.

In one of my favourite endings of any **Doctor Who** story, the Doctor makes his goodbyes so he can get back to his own laboratory and his work on the TARDIS, but there's still plenty to be done at Space Centre. They have to send up another rocket and arrange an exchange with the aliens, in order to get the Earth astronauts back home. In a moment that never fails to delight, the Doctor's response to being asked for more help is, 'Here's Miss Shaw, she's much more practical than I am.'[88] And with that acknowledgement, the Doctor is off; leaving humanity to sink or swim on its own merits, now that the crisis and the mystery are over.

---

[88] Episode seven.

BIBLIOGRAPHY

Books

Conan Doyle, Arthur, *The Penguin Complete Sherlock Holmes*. London, Penguin Books Ltd, 2009. ISBN 9780141040288.

Dicks, Terrance, *Doctor Who: The Ambassadors of Death*. **The Target Doctor Who Library** #121. London, WH Allen, 1987. ISBN 9780491034234.

Hill, CN, *A Vertical Empire: The History of the UK Rocket and Space Programme, 1950-1971*. London, Imperial College Press, 2012. ISBN 9781848167957.

Parkin, Lance, *Lance Parkin*. **Time Unincorporated: The Doctor Who Fanzine Archives** #1. Des Moines, Mad Norwegian Press, 2009. ISBN 9781935234012.

Periodicals

Parkin, Lance, 'Something Took Off From Mars…'. Matrix #52, Spring 1998. In *Lance Parkin*, pp95-99.

Television

The Avengers. Associated British Corporation, 1961-69.

Batman. 20th Century Fox Television, Greenway Productions, 1966-68.

Doctor Who. BBC, 1963-.

The Man from UNCLE. Arena Productions, MGM Television, 1964-68.

The Professionals. London Weekend Television, Mark 1 Productions, 1977-1983.

The Quatermass Experiment. BBC, 1953.

Quatermass II. BBC, 1955.

Quatermass and the Pit. BBC, 1958-59.

Star Trek. Desilu Productions, Norway Corporation, Paramount Television, 1966-69.

    The Doomsday Machine, 1967.

The Sweeney. Euston Films, Thames Television, 1975-78.

Torchwood. BBC Wales, BBC Worldwide, Canadian Broadcasting Corporation, Starz Entertainment, 2006-11.

Yes Minister. BBC, 1980-84.

Yes, Prime Minister. BBC, 1986-88.

Film

Kubrick, Stanley, dir, *2001: A Space Odyssey*. MGM, Stanley Kubrick Productions, 1968.

Websites

Dan Dare and the Eagle. http://www.dandare.org/. Accessed 8 January 2016.

European Space Agency. http://www.esa.int/ESA.

    'A Look at the Past'. 11 December 2012. http://www.esa.int/our_activities/launchers/a_look_at_the _past2. Accessed 8 January 2016.

'Ariane 4'. 14 May 2004.
http://www.esa.int/our_activities/launchers/ariane_42.
Accessed 8 January 2016.

'Ariane 5'. 11 November 2015.
http://www.esa.int/our_activities/launchers/launch_vehicle
s/ariane_5. Accessed 8 January 2016.

'History: Hermes Spaceplane, 1987'.
http://www.esa.int/About_Us/Welcome_to_ESA/ESA_histor
y/History_Hermes_spaceplane_1987. Accessed 8 January
2016.

'Orion'.
http://www.esa.int/Our_Activities/Human_Spaceflight/High
lights/Orion. Accessed 8 January 2016.

'Freudian Trio'. TV Tropes.
http://tvtropes.org/pmwiki/pmwiki.php/Main/FreudianTrio.
Accessed 8 January 2016.

'Gender Bias without Borders'. Geena Davis Institute on Gender in
Media. http://seejane.org/symposiums-on-gender-in-
media/gender-bias-without-borders/. Accessed 8 January 2016.

Bolton, Paul, 'Education: Historical Statistics – November 2012'. 27
November 2012. Digital Education Resource Archive.
http://dera.ioe.ac.uk/22771/. Accessed 8 January 2016.

Davis, Geena, 'Geena Davis' Two Easy Steps to Make Hollywood
Less Sexist (Guest Column)'. *Hollywood Reporter*, 11 December
2013. http://www.hollywoodreporter.com/news/geena-davis-two-
easy-steps-664573. Accessed 8 January 2016.

Sullivan, Shannon Patrick, 'The Ambassadors of Death'. *A Brief History of Time (Travel)*.
http://www.shannonsullivan.com/drwho/serials/ccc.html. Accessed 8 January 2016.

BIOGRAPHY

L M Myles is a Scottish writer, editor, and podcaster. She co-edited the Hugo-Award-nominated anthology *Chicks Unravel Time* (with Deborah Stanish), and *Companion Piece* (with Liz Barr). She's written for **Doctor Who** in prose and on audio, most recently in *The Scientific Secrets of Doctor Who*; and she's the co-host of the Hugo-nominated podcast *Verity!* and the **Blake's 7** podcast *Down and Safe*, which she also produces.